Advance Praise for

Contemporary Anarchist Criminology

"This book is a much-needed defense of the work we do nationally in ending the incarceration of all youth and promoting transformative justice."

—Madelynne Kinoshita, *Save the Kids*

"The editors and authors in *Contemporary Anarchist Criminology* are unwavering in their fearlessness to throw bold punches at authority and convention. Where many may not understand, their approaches and position deserve careful consideration in these most uncertain times."

—David Stovall, Professor of African-American Studies and Educational Policy Studies, University of Illinois at Chicago

"A must-read book for those who know the criminal justice system is broken, and want a solution. The editors and contributors present an anarchist theory of criminology, sure to challenge the failings of the criminal justice system for decades to come."

—Amber E. George, Editor, *Journal for Critical Animal Studies*

"*Contemporary Anarchist Criminology* is a brilliant, insightful, and uncompromising collection, which both empowers and inspires the reader in equal measure. First, by provoking an urgently needed critical reading of the deep and inherent failings of orthodox judicial systems to come to the fore. Second, through advancing a range of persuasive arguments for anarchist criminologies to underpin new visions, and animate new ways-of-beings, in order to usher in new forms of social justice into the world. Crucially, these radical expressions of social justice, rooted as many are in intersectional resistance movements, and steeped in a politics of total liberation, are always in existence far removed from the twin tyrannies of capital and state. In short, this book makes a powerful and timely intervention into the existing literature, and deserves to be read widely."

—Richard J. White, Reader in Human Geography, Sheffield Hallam University, United Kingdom

"We live in increasingly illiberal times. According to the CIVICUS 'State of Civil Society Report' for 2017, only 3% of the world's people live in nation-states where civic space is fully open. There is a need to look for alternative intellectual and institutional models that will increase the space for broader public engagement, allowing for the attainment of greater social justice. *Contemporary Anarchist Criminology* contributes significantly to this search, introducing readers to a range of voices, ideas, and arguments, many of them with a long lineage, and yet seldom heard within the mainstream of conventional wisdom regarding our criminal justice system. The introductory chapter by the editors, plus the nine chapters by various contributors, including present-day prisoners, offer a compelling critique of current ideologies, policies, and practices, while furnishing humane and doable paths for action."

—A. Peter Castro, Associate Professor of Anthropology and Robert D. McClure Professor of Teaching Excellence, Maxwell School for Citizenship and Public Affairs, Syracuse University

"This valuable collection presents a strong critique of structures of oppression and injustice. It introduces important new perspectives that are vital for building a critical criminology and for creating much-needed radical transformation."

—John Sorenson, Professor, Department of Sociology, Brock University

"Finally, the first book on anarchist criminology!! What took so long. Now can we have prison abolition? A must read for anyone that cares about people."

—Editorial Board, *Poetry Behind the Walls*

"A straightforward short important text to begin the movement for anarchist criminology. This text does not strive to discuss every issue that could be possibly discussed, but rather says here is the first book on the topic; now everyone go out and write and organize."

—*Green Theory and Praxis Journal*

Contemporary Anarchist Criminology

RADICAL ANIMAL STUDIES
AND TOTAL LIBERATION

Anthony J. Nocella II
Series Editor

Vol. 6

The Radical Animal Studies and Total Liberation series
is part of the Peter Lang Education list.
Every volume is peer reviewed and meets
the highest quality standards for content and production.

PETER LANG
New York • Bern • Berlin
Brussels • Vienna • Oxford • Warsaw

Contemporary Anarchist Criminology

Against Authoritarianism and Punishment

Anthony J. Nocella II,
Mark Seis,
Jeff Shantz,
EDITORS

PETER LANG
New York • Bern • Berlin
Brussels • Vienna • Oxford • Warsaw

Library of Congress Cataloging-in-Publication Data

Names: Nocella, Anthony J., editor. | Seis, Mark C., editor.
Shantz, Jeff, editor.
Title: Contemporary anarchist criminology: against authoritarianism and punishment / Anthony J. Nocella II, Mark Seis, and Jeff Shantz, editors.
Description: New York: Peter Lang, 2018.
Series: Radical animal studies and total liberation; vol. 6
ISSN 2469-3065 (print) | ISSN 2469-3081 (online)
Includes bibliographical references and index.
Identifiers: LCCN 2018021042 | ISBN 978-1-4331-5800-1 (hardback: alk. paper)
ISBN 978-1-4331-5804-9 (paperback: alk. paper) | ISBN 978-1-4331-5801-8 (ebook pdf)
ISBN 978-1-4331-5802-5 (epub) | ISBN 978-1-4331-5803-2 (mobi)
Subjects: LCSH: Criminology. | Anarchism. | Criminal justice, Administration of.
Classification: LCC HV6030 .C675 | DDC 364—dc23
LC record available at https://lccn.loc.gov/2018021042
DOI 10.3726/b14254

Bibliographic information published by **Die Deutsche Nationalbibliothek**.
Die Deutsche Nationalbibliothek lists this publication in the "Deutsche Nationalbibliografie"; detailed bibliographic data are available on the Internet at http://dnb.d-nb.de/.

29 Broadway, 18th floor, New York, NY 10006
www.peterlang.com

This book is dedicated to all of those who resist and work to destroy power, authority, punishment, domination, and oppression. This book is also dedicated to all of those that have been exploited, tortured, and murdered in the name of control, punishment, and domination. This book is dedicated to those that want revolution and not reform.

Contents

Foreword

LUIS A. FERNANDEZ

The world is once again in turmoil. In the last decade, we witnessed a capitalist economic crisis that increased financial inequality and burden the working class disproportionally. We saw the carceral state continue to grow and administer disproportionate levels of punishment and repression toward communities of color. Yet, we also experienced large protest movements across the globe. For the first time in decades, riots returned in inner cities as a form of protest. And strong resistance movements arose in the United States and Europe, including Occupy and Black Lives Matter. More recently, and in response to these counter movements, we see a re-emergence of white supremacy and fascist ideologies embraced at multiple levels of our society. Add to all this we see a targeted and sustained effort to deport undocumented people. Given this, it is not hyperbolic to suggest that we are living in uncertain times. As a result, Contemporary Anarchist Criminology is all the more relevant, with the authors taking aim at the root causes of our crisis that is embedded in the law, power, and authority itself.

Unlike many of you reading this book, I became aware of anarchism relatively late, and did not fully comprehend the connection of anarchism to criminology until my doctoral work. In 2003, I found myself at Word Trade Organization (WTO) meetings in Cancun, Mexico, along with 10,000 other protesters from all over the globe. Present were campesinos, farmers, indigenous people from Latin America, and anarchists from Italy, Argentina, Mexico, France, and the United States. All were resisting a global neoliberal forces that, at the time, were trying to eliminate food security across the world in one swoop. Watching these groups assemble in parks, make collective decisions, engage in mutual aid, and launch an effective counter attack, all while speaking multiple languages, demonstrated the power of an anti-authoritarian model of organizing.

Since my experience in 2003, I embraced the anarchist tradition, mainly because of its uncompromising critique of the law, power, and the state. For example, I have organized closely with undocumented people (mostly women who do janitorial work in hotels) to fight the legal onslaught brought against them in Arizona. Immigration laws developed in the mid-2000s were designed to make the lives of undocumented people untenable, aiming to eliminate access to health care, education, work, and even the ability to rent a house. These efforts toward untenability are now common in various states, having re-emerged nation-wide with the recent calls to "build a wall". For almost a decade, a group of us (documented and undocumented) met on a weekly basis to analyze and strategize on how to build a successful collective response. Reflecting a bit of what I saw in Cancun, Mexico, our meetings are bilingual, non-hierarchical, and resemble an assembly as much as possible. Partly based on anarchist critiques of power and authority, the group directly challenged the disproportional influences of local hotel owners on city and state regulations regarding wages and immigration status. The group understands that these hotel owners benefit economically from harsh immigration laws, since these laws suppress labor costs and attempts to scare undocumented people from complaining about their work environments. As such, individuals in the group often described being threatened with respect to challenging wage theft and feared managers' threats to call immigration law enforcement on them and their families. Through discussion and their lived experiences, the workers we organized with often understood the discriminating bias of the law and the abusive application of power, all without academic lectures or explanations. After a decade, this group continues to fight for everyone's right to live, love, and work wherever they please.

I did not arrive at my community and scholarly work on my own. Rather, there were great thinkers who helped me along the way. Some of those thinkers are in this book. As you will see, *Contemporary Anarchist Criminology* contains classical articles that will help you formulate ideas, giving a conceptual background that can form the foundation for decades worth of work. Just to point to a couple of examples, Jeff Ferrell, Harold E. Pepinsky and Jeff Shantz chapters alone present strong foundational concepts to anarchist criminology. The quickly present critiques to classical criminology conceptions and point to solutions to criminological problems through decentralized, collaborative, and community embedded approaches. Reading the rest of the book, you may notice that anarchist criminology has loose borders, encompassing a link to a variety of other theoretical approaches such as feminism, abolitionism, radical ecology and radical criminology. Yet, anarchist criminology has a long history, one linked to robust tradition of anarchist thinking. This history gives the ideas and practice contained in the volume a depth and breadth that will be useful to people embarking in anarchist criminological thought.

I invite the reader to join me in engaging the ideas in this volume. At this historical juncture, in the middle of a serious political crisis, accompanied with a rise in white nationalism, *Contemporary Anarchist Criminology* points toward a different kind of future. Perhaps a future where we eliminate incarceration, abolish subjugation, engage in direct democracy, build autonomous spaces, and pursue equality with a fervor of our intellectual ancestors.

See you in the streets.

Acknowledgements

This book could not be possible without the support of our families, friends, and the Earth. We would like to thank all of the amazing contributors Jeff Ferrell, Harold Pepinsky, Colleen Hackett, Ben Turk, Laura Magnani, Reverend David "Wolf Eyes" Rose, Sr., Maurice L. Graham, and Sean Swain. We would also like to thank Sarah Bode, Sara McBride and everyone at Peter Lang. Finally, we would like to thank everyone that wrote a review for the books prior to it coming out, Green Theory and Praxis Journal, Poetry Behind the Walls Editorial Board, Madelynne Kinoshita, Marissa Anderson, David Stovall, John Sorenson, Peter Castro, Amber E. George, and Richard J. White. We would also like to thank all the anarchist and social justice collectives and organization that are excited for the book to come and want to promote it on their social media.

Introduction: The Rise of Anarchist Criminology

ANTHONY J. NOCELLA II, MARK SEIS, AND JEFF SHANTZ

This is a period of open social war. The stakes for analyzing, understanding, responding to, and changing relations of power are high. Criminal justice systems and their institutions are the front lines of struggles over social injustices and the pursuit of social justice. Movements and organizations like Idle No More, Black Lives Matter, Antifa, Jericho Movement, Critical Resistance, Youth Justice Coalition, Save the Kids, Earth Liberation Front, Animal Liberation Front, Standing Rock, No One Is Illegal, the movements for Missing and Murdered Indigenous Women and Girls, openly contest and oppose criminal justice systems based on exploitation, oppression, repression and pose promising alternatives. Anarchist former political prisoner and former Black Panther, Ashanti Alston (n.a.) explains the problems of the state:

> I AM AN ANARCHIST WHO BELIEVES… that "The State" is inherently oppressive as a mechanism that cannot GIVE, GRANT, GUARANTEE OR PRESERVE Freedom, or make revolutionary change.
>
> Without the state, anarchy has existed in varying forms since the earliest human social formations, because anarchists believe that people can govern their own lives, individually and collectively, based on commonly worked out and agreed upon visions, interests, mutual aid, non-hierarchical decision-making, codes of conduct, open collaborative theories and plans for direct and democratic control of the means of livelihood, and people's power to bring about prosperity, peace, harmony, fun, adventure, protection, nurturance and an atmosphere for spiritually wholistic well-being without adherence to private property, money, god, race supremacy, able-bodied supremacy, age-ism, imperialism, etc. (http://www.anarchistpanther.net/, para. 34 and 25)

Alston's article is an intersectional revolutionary understanding, explaining to activists how all movements and all forms of oppression are connected.

Criminology as the analysis of the state and its criminal justice systems plays a part in this critique. And, in contrast to what some might want to believe, it does, and must, take sides. The state is not neutral nor can criminology be neutral. While too much of criminology perhaps takes the side of power and control, there are rich histories of criminology that side with the exploited and oppressed. Anarchist criminology has been foremost among those perspectives that side with the oppressed and exploited against the oppressors and exploiters and which pose new ways of relating, new forms of justice (beyond and against the state and capital).

Here from the Start

Despite what orthodox histories of criminology would have us believe, anarchism has been present and active from the very beginning within the discipline. And indeed, anarchism provided some of the sharpest and most insightful analyses of crime and criminal justice systems as part of social systems. Anarchism also provided some of the strongest and most sustained criticisms of orthodox criminological research and theories, such as Lombroso's work. And despite what dominant theory texts would present to students, anarchist criminology has maintained an active and engaged contribution to criminological thought. This can be seen from the works of Peter Kropotkin and Emma Goldman early on through the works of C. Wright Mills in the 1950s and 1960s through early influences on Jock Young right up to the current resurgence of anarchist criminology and the contributions included in this volume (Guerin, 2005). If anything, anarchist criminology has provided a major impetus for the revitalization of critical and radical criminology after a down period during the political reaction of the 1980s and 1990s (not only reflected in the dominance of broken windows but in the Left Realist and postmodern capitulations among progressives).

As the chapters in this collection show very clearly, anarchist criminology is diverse, vital, and energetic. It offers cutting analysis of social structures of inequity, oppression, exploitation, and injustice as well as the parts played by criminal justice systems and their institutions in these social realities. At the same time anarchist criminology points to meaningful alternatives to present systems and goes beyond so-called pragmatic concerns with limited reforms to show that radical transformation is realistic and possible (Shantz, 2013).

Anarchist criminology is not limited by the pragmatism of lowered expectations or the limits of a realism that refuses to see that social movements, radical alternatives, and resistance are also very much part of current reality and have been all along (Shantz & Macdonald, 2013). Anarchist criminology has influenced important developments in criminology, from transformative justice to abolition, to decriminalization, to harm reduction (Davis, 2003; Fernandez, 2008; Nocella II, 2011; Pepinsky, 2006). All of these influences put an emphasis on mutual aid and solidarity rather than control and command. Anarchist criminology is about building inclusive liberating communities interwoven with the global ecological world, rooted in direct democracy, not governments, bosses, laws, nonprofit organizations, capitalism, and corporations even if they are striving to be more responsible or greener (Best & Nocella II, 2006). Anarchist criminology is not only about abolition and smashing the state, but about transformative holistic alternatives, which promote healing and accountability. Anarchist criminology is moving away from state representations of restorative justice. Restorative justice, unlike transformative justice, supports the current criminal justice system and there are some restorative justice practitioners who support the death penalty. Transformative justice, unlike restorative justice, advocates for police, prison, and punishment abolition. Transformative justice, unlike restorative justice, is anti-state, anti-academic industrial complex, anti-capitalist, and anti-oppression and advocates for non-violent revolution, direct democracy, and identity politics (Nocella II, 2012). Anarchist criminology is about radical transformative liberation, not reform (Nocella II, White, & Cudworth, 2015).

Anarchism has always been diverse—both in assessment of the state and capital and in terms of prescriptions for social change (Amster, DeLeon, Fernandez, Nocella II, & Shannon, 2009). Anarchists have also pursued freedom through diverse means—collectivism, communism, insurrection, etc. (Shantz, 2011). Some emphasize individual liberty while others focus on collective freedom. All generally agree that individuals and collectives, and their freedoms, are intertwined. The present collection shows the diversity of anarchist concerns and perspectives.

A Criminology for Social Transformation

Anarchism is first and foremost a movement for social transformation. It is rooted in the struggles of the oppressed and exploited (Kropotkin, 2002). Anarchist criminology is and has always been connected to real world movements for freedom and liberty. Anarchist criminology is always for social justice. This gives anarchist criminology its vibrancy and its relevance.

It also means that anarchist criminology has never been strictly a scholarly or academic practice (Guerin, 1970). Rather it is rooted in, arises from, and is developed through social experiences. It is practical (of practice) and experiential—words that have gained growing recognition within social sciences recently. It also means that the alternatives and solutions to address social problems identified and proposed by anarchist criminologists have a basis in real world experiences, concerns, and outcomes. This occurs in ways that orthodox criminology tends not to, particularly in relation to the experiences of the criminalized and punished.

It goes without saying that anarchist criminology does not look to the state or its criminal justice systems for solutions—seeing them rather as making up much of the problem in the first place. This means anarchists eschew easy answers and solutions that are too often unquestioned—taken for granted as they are. Anarchists have seen the institutions of so-called justice as being fundamental sources of injustice, and many anarchists know the injustices up close and in person. They recognize that what is called crime is more accurately difference, resistance, or simply survival (outside of means legitimized by economic, political, or cultural powerholders) (Shannon, Nocella II, & Asimakopoulous, 2012). Anarchists challenge us all to ask what crime really is and who gets to decide? (Avrich, 2005).

State Violence

Not insignificantly, anarchists have disproportionately suffered the violence of the state and criminal justice systems. Anarchists have often been the targets of cultural forms of regulation in what we might now call moral panics or what was once simply constructed as deviance (or degeneracy or delinquency) (Berkman, 2003). Notably, Kropotkin and Goldman were criminalized, imprisoned, and deported. An anarchist worker wrote one of the earliest criticisms of Lombroso from a prison cell, arrested for union organizing during the Haymarket police riot that Lombroso exploited for his own ends. The anarchist punks of the 1980s sparked moral panics and more recently the black bloc of the twenty-first century have been called hooligans and terrorists (Nocella II, 2013).

The Industrial Workers of the World (IWW) always said of political prisoners: "We're in here for you. You're out there for us." Anarchists have maintained connections to prisoners who are always part of anarchist movements. Anarchist criminologists have a greater proportion of members who have been criminalized and made prisoners.

For an Insurgent Criminology

Anarchists have also recognized and supported organic or insurgent criminologies rooted in and developed through resistance movements. Anarchists today note that some of the most pointed and incisive analyses are coming from resistance movements, from Idle No More, Black Lives Matter, Save the Kids, Antifa, Earth Liberation Front, Animal Liberation Front, No One Is Illegal, Standing Rock, and the movements for Missing and Murdered Indigenous Women and Girls, to name only a few. Anarchist criminology comes from these movements and/or is informed by them. Anarchism seeks to break down barriers between campus and community. Organizations like the Critical Criminology Working Group at Kwantlen Polytechnic University and Save the Kids both show radical organizing among formal criminologists and campus-based resistance in action and solidarity with community movements.

Anarchist criminology is a criminology that is defiantly for communities, not of and for criminal justice systems and the current order of things. The communities that give rise to and sustain resistance provide the impetus for alternatives (Abu-Jamal, 2000). Anarchist criminology shows the contributions that criminological research, scholarship, theory, and action can make to resistance and rethinking social arrangements. It shifts analytical focus away from the blaming of the working class and poor to demonstrate that the real social harms come from states and capital. And ending major social harms means ending states and capital (and their representatives in policing, prisons, speculation, and ownership, etc.). Against a discipline that takes the state for granted and legitimizes criminal justice systems, anarchism prioritizes the voices of those targeted and harmed by the state. Anarchist criminology recognizes criminal justice systems as outcomes of specific power structures, not as natural or legitimate social institutions (the so-called best of all possible worlds) which cannot be abolished and replaced with much better. The present collection shows the diversity of anarchist concerns and perspectives.

Overview of the Book

The first part of this collection re-situates anarchism within criminology. It offers a rereading of criminology and sets the stage for a serious reconsideration of anarchism in and as criminology.

In Chapter 1, "Against the Law: Anarchist Criminology," Jeff Ferrell notes that anarchist criminology disrupts and disorients taken for granted assumptions of the discipline. It challenges common sense views that, pretending to be "reasonable," keep us locked within status quo arrangements of power and authority and instead offers some alternatives as resistance. Jeff Ferrell's work since the 1990s has done much to return anarchism to the center of debates in criminology.

In Chapter 2, "Communist Anarchism as an Alternative to the Rule of Criminal Law," Harold Pepinsky finds one useful alternative in anarchist communism. Compulsion and the state offer no solutions to crime. People in society need to be empowered. Pepinsky's chapter is a call to rethink both classical criminology and anarchism.

In Chapter 3, "Lombroso and the Anarchists: Anarchism in the Formation of Criminology," Jeff Shantz provides a further rethinking of the origins and development of criminology. Shantz looks at the overlooked place of anarchism in the history of criminology through an analysis of the works of Cesare Lombroso, who developed his theories in the service of repressing anarchist resistance.

In Part II, Chapters 4–6 provide detailed discussions of alternatives to criminal justice systems from the perspectives of anarchism. Key among these are abolitionist approaches.

In Chapter 4, "'Freedom First': Pursuing Abolition Through Supporting Prisoner Resistance," Colleen Hackett and Ben Turk focus on prisoners' resistance as a starting point for opposition and alternatives to, the capitalist, patriarchal, white supremacist state. Prisoners' efforts provide material and theoretical contributions to abolitionist perspectives and actions. The goal is to make prisons socially impossible.

In Chapter 5, "From Prison Abolition to Transformative Justice," Laura Magnani notes that it is not enough to demonstrate the failure of the prison system. There is a need to rethink all aspects of statist criminal justice. Transformative justice would not restore repressive structures but rather replace them.

In Chapter 6, "An Anarchist Criminology for Understanding Environmental Degradation," Mark Seis shifts the focus of criminology away from the domain of street crime to address the more impactful and destructive crimes against our planet. Seis shows that we must move beyond illusions of regulation within a capitalist framework. Rather we require a transformative ecological justice guided by anarchist principles of mutual aid.

Part III offers prisoner voices as integral parts of anarchist criminology. Anarchism returns prisoners to active makers of criminological theory and practice.

In Chapter 7, "The Staff of Chronos," Reverend David "Wolf Eyes" Rose Sr., outlines how the United States prison system reproduces itself as an economic concern. He too shows the actual reasonableness of transformative justice and its necessity if we are really concerned with addressing social harms rather than simply expanding them.

In Chapter 8, "Actual Connections to Slavery in the Prison System," Maurice L. Graham shows the ongoing connections with the prison system and slavery in the United States. Slavery never went away in the United States, was never abolished. And Graham demonstrates the many legal survivals of the Confederacy.

In Chapter 9, "On Crime and Deviance," Sean Swain asks the reader to fundamentally rethink notions of crime itself. Crime is an outcome of claims of rulership. From a consistently anarchist perspective we cannot address crime until we address, and eliminate rulership. Indeed, much of what is called crime, and the focus of criminology, is not especially harmful, which much of what harms society (colonialism, pollution, exploitation, eco-destruction, etc.) is not criminalized or given attention by criminology.

This book is not the be all and final text on anarchist criminology; it is far from it. It is a short, concise text designed to aid in the development of a complex field of anarchist criminological study focused on alternative structures of organization and resistance movements. This text is not as inclusive as we would like it to be and it lacks a global focus. Also, the text needs more authors representing more diverse viewpoints from the spectrum of human experiences of resistance and struggle. We would like to have had more indigenous voices along with chapters dedicated to other oppressed groups such as, but not limited to disability, LGBTTQQIA+, Hip Hop, punk, and Southeast Asian, African, South and Central America, and youth. Hopefully, this text can get the dialogue going and rectify the need for more diversity in the development of a theoretically sound anarchist criminology.

References

Abu-Jamal, M. (2000). *All things censored.* New York, NY: Seven Stories Press.

Alston, A. (n.a.). *One journey into and out of the anarchist ... BLACK!* Retrieved November 20, 2017 from http://www.anarchistpanther.net/

Amster, R., DeLeon, A. P., Fernandez, L. A., Nocella II, A. J., & Shannon, D. (2009). *Contemporary anarchist studies: An introductory anthology of anarchy in the academy.* Edited Book. New York, NY: Routledge.

Avrich, P. (2005). *Anarchist voices.* Oakland, CA: AK Press.

Berkman, A. (2003). *What is anarchism?* Oakland, CA: AK Press.

Best, S., & Nocella II, A. J. (2006). *Igniting a revolution: Voices in defense of the Earth.* Oakland, CA: AK Press.

Davis, A.Y. (2003). *Are prisons obsolete?* New York, NY: Seven Stories Press.

Fernandez, L. A. (2008). *Policing dissent: Social control and the anti-globalization movement.* Piscataway, NJ: Rutgers University Press.

Guerin, D. (1970). *Anarchism: From theory to practice.* New York, NY: Monthly Review Press.

Guerin, D. (2005). *No gods no masters: An anthology of anarchism.* Oakland, CA: AK Press.

Kropotkin, P. (2002). *Anarchism: A collection of revolutionary writings.* Mineola, NY: Dover Publications.

Nocella II, A. J. (2012). An overview of the history and theory of transformative justice. *Peace & Conflict Review, 6*(1), 1–10.

Nocella II, A. J. (2013). The rise of the terrorization of dissent. In M. E. Nagel & A. J. Nocella II (Eds.), *The end of prisons: Reflections from the decarceration movement* (pp. 13–30). New York, NY: Rodopi.

Nocella II, A. J., White, R., & Cudworth, E. (2015). *Anarchism and animal liberation: Essays on complementary elements of total liberation.* Jefferson, NC: McFarland.

Pepinsky, H. E. (2006). *Peacemaking: Reflections of a radical criminologist.* Ottawa, CA: University of Ottawa Press.

Shannon, D., Nocella II, A. J., & Asimakopoulous, J. (2012). *The accumulation of freedom: Writings on anarchist economics.* Oakland, CA: AK Press.

Shantz, J. (2011). *Against all authority: Anarchism and the literary imagination.* Upton Pyne: Imprint Academic.

Shantz, J. (2013). *Commonist tendencies: Mutual aid beyond communism.* Goleta, CA: Punctum Books.

Shantz, J., & Macdonald, J. B. (2013). *Beyond capitalism: Building democratic alternatives for today and the future.* New York, NY: Bloomsbury Publishing.

Part I
Contemporary Classics on Anarchist Criminology

1. *Against the Law: Anarchist Criminology*

JEFF FERRELL

Anarchism is an orientation toward social life and social relations that is ultimately no orientation at all. In fact, anarchism might best be thought of as a disorientation; that is, an approach which openly values fractured, uncertain, and unrealized understandings and practices as the emerging essence of social life. What follows, then, is guaranteed to be an incomplete account of anarchism and anarchist criminology, a failed attempt at orientation. This failure certainly derives from the account's origins in the work of a single author, and from that author, like others, being caught up in the dementia of deadlines and daily work. But it also derives from the nature of anarchism itself. Like most all theoretical or practical models, anarchism incorporates a variety of limitations and contradictions (Feyerabend, 1975). Unlike most other orientations, anarchism acknowledges and celebrates these failings, and doesn't bother to hide them behind cloaks of absolute certainty or competence.

Unlike most modernist intellectual orientations, anarchism and anarchist criminology don't bother pretending to incorporate reasoned or reasonable critiques of law and legal authority, either. In fact, to the extent that the legal and cultural machinery of the modern nation state, and the accumulated experiences of daily life under such regimes of power, construct "reason" and a sense of what is reasonable, anarchists and anarchist criminologists argue that progressive social change requires the "unreasonable" and the "unthinkable." In other words, to the degree that reason and "common sense" help keep us locked within present arrangements of authority and power, it seems in our interest to stop making sense, to imagine the unimaginable. Beyond this, as will be seen, anarchists and anarchist criminologists also launch aggressive and "unreasonable" critiques against law and legal authority because they see time and again that such authority undermines human community and constrains human diversity. Unlike some other critical or progressive criminologies, then, anarchist criminology stands not as a careful criticism of criminal justice, a "loyal opposition" to the state and state law. It stands instead as a disloyal and disrespectful (Mazor, 1978) attack, a "counterpunch to the belly of authority" (Ferrell, 1996). As the Industrial Workers of the World (The Wobblies)—a free-swinging anarchist labor union of the early twentieth century—said: "We are not 'undesirable citizens.' We are not citizens at all. We are rebellious slaves ....Therefore we are not respectable. We admit it and we are proud of it" (Industrial Worker, 1912).

In promoting fluid and uncertain social relations, and attacking the sorts of legal authority which stifle them, anarchist criminology aims its disrespectable gaze both high and low. Anarchist criminology arrogantly assaults the structures of state and legal authority ensconced above us; but it also humbly encourages all those below and beyond this authority who invent ways of resisting it, and imagines with them a host of unreasonable and egalitarian alternatives. With H. L. Mencken, anarchist criminology seeks to afflict those comfortable with legal power and privilege, and to comfort those afflicted by its abuses.

Against the Law: Through the Past, Darkly

Anarchist critiques of law and legality, and thus the roots of contemporary anarchist criminology, trace as far as anarchism itself. Early anarchist writers and activists like William Godwin (1756–1836), Max Stirner (1806–1856), Michael Bakunin (1814–1876), and Peter Kropotkin (1842–1921) focused some of their most scathing and sophisticated attacks on state authority and legal control. Godwin (1971) for example argued that "whatever inconveniences may arise from the passions of men <sic>, the introduction of fixed laws cannot be the genuine remedy," in that such laws tend "to fix the human mind in a stagnant condition," to inhibit lived solutions to human problems, and to promote state-administered "criminal justice" and punishment. Kropotkin (1975) likewise critiqued the law's "tendency to crystallize what should be modified and developed day by day," but went further to call for the abolition of prisons—"monuments of human hypocrisy and cowardice" which promote rather than prevent criminality—and for the destruction of state law itself: "In place of the cowardly phrase, 'Obey the law,' our cry is 'Revolt against all laws!'" Similarly, Stirner (1971) called for "war ... against establishment itself, the State"—for the state to be "abrogated, annihilated, done away with, not reformed"—and argued that crime in this context constituted a sort of individualistic rebellion against state law and authority. But perhaps Bakunin (1974), in calling for the destruction of the state and its replacement with "the spontaneous and continuous action of the masses, the groups and the associations of people," presented the twisted potential of the anarchist attack on state law most succinctly: "The passion for destruction is a creative passion, too."

Appropriately, anarchist critiques such as these have emerged not just as theoretical statements, but out of head-on confrontations between state legal authorities and anarchists attempting to construct alternative arrangements. Especially for Bakunin and Kropotkin, anarchist criminology was part of revolutionary activity against the Russian oligarchy and the emerging nation states of capitalism. In fact, Bakunin's notion of "the spontaneous and continuous action of the masses" referred to an actual case of anarchist revolt: the Paris Commune of 1871. In the U. S., anarchists like Emma Goldman (1869–1940) and Alexander Berkman (1870–1936) likewise mixed labor and social activism with insightful critiques—see for example Goldman's (1969) essay "Prisons: A Social Crime and Failure"—and spent large periods of their own time in prison for their trouble. Most remarkable were the Wobblies. The Wobblies blended deceptive strategies to avoid legal prosecution with out-and-out defiance of the law; as their national newspaper, the Industrial Worker (1913), put it: "Damn the laws of the ruling class. We will have none of them. Capitalist law and order means law forced upon the workers by order of the capitalists." But beyond deception and defiance, the Wobblies and their allied unions also invented strategies that could successfully turn the turgidity of the law against itself, and thus win for them labor and political victories. In the workplace, they at times obeyed every rule and regulation so precisely as to finally grind all work to a halt; in the streets, they systematically violated unjust laws in such great numbers as to overload courts and jails, and force dismissal of their cases (Ferrell, 1991; Ferrell & Ryan, 1985; Kornbluh, 1988).

Anarchist criminology's uncertain trajectory of course continues into the present as well. In fact, the past few decades have seen an efflorescence of anarchist criminology. In 1974, the membership of the American Society for Political and Legal Philosophy for some odd reason "voted overwhelmingly for 'anarchism'" as the topic for their national meeting, and a book of essays on anarchism, law, and justice (Pennock & Chapman, 1978) followed in 1978. That same year, criminologist Harold Pepinsky (1978) published an article advocating "communist anarchism as an alternative to the rule of criminal law," and later transformed this approach into a "peacemaking criminology" (Pepinsky, 1991; Pepinsky & Jesilow, 1984; Pepinsky & Quinney, 1991) opposed to the violence inherent in the concept and practice of state law. Around this same time, criminologist Larry Tifft (1979; Tifft & Sullivan, 1980) developed an anarchist criminology which argued for replacing state/legal "justice" with a fluid, face-to-face form of justice grounded in emerging human needs. More recently, Bruce DiCristina (1995; Ferrell, 1995a) has constructed a critique of criminology and criminal justice from the work of anarchist philosopher of science Paul Feyerabend (1975). And I (Ferrell 1994, 1995a, 1995b, 1996; Ryan & Ferrell, 1986) have developed an anarchist criminology aimed especially at examining the interplay between state/legal authority, day-to-day resistance to it, and the practice of criminality.

As before, though, contemporary anarchist attacks on state legality and control continue to emerge also out of non-academic realms. In 1968, a century after the Paris Commune, French "Situationists" spurred on an anarchist revolt against the centralized French governmental and economic system with slogans like "Work Is The Blackmail of Existence" and "Boredom Is Always Counterrevolutionary." Beginning in the late 1970s, and in the Situationist politics of its founders, the British and U.S. punk movement likewise promoted "DIY"—do-it-yourself—in place of outside authority and control. From bands like the Sex Pistols ("Anarchy in the U.K.") and The Clash ("Working for the Clampdown," "Guns of Brixton," "Know Your Rights") to Rancid ("11th Hour," "Time Bomb," "As Wicked"), the punks have continued to promote anarcho-critical understandings of state law and state injustice as well. During the 1990s, outlaw anarchist radio stations like Free Radio Berkeley (Ongerth & Radio Free Berkeley, 1995) have not only broadcast punk and other alternative music, but have defied FCC regulations to broadcast programs like "Copwatch" and "The First Amendment Show."

And there is more—more illegal "micro-power" stations hidden all around the country, more punks and prisoners with critical and "unwholesome" attitudes toward authority, more people whose day-to-day disavowals of state legality lie outside my knowledge and perhaps that of most others as well. This is, or course, exactly as it should be. Anarchism and anarchist criminology constitute less a closed intellectual system administered by a handful of experts than a critical undercurrent in which everyone may or may not be caught. And in this sense, anarchism and anarchist criminology exist as part of a long and dark "secret history" (Marcus, 1989) of resistance, moving underground by force or by choice, and always flowing under and against state and legal authority.

Against the Law: The Spiraling Harm of Criminalization and Legal Control

Anarchist criminology certainly incorporates the sort of "visceral revolt"(-Guerin, 1970) that characterizes anarchism itself, the passionate sense of "fuck authority," to quote the old anarchist slogan, that comes from being shoved around by police officers, judges, bosses, priests, and other authorities one time too many. Moreover, anarchists would agree with many feminist and postmodernist theorists that such visceral passions matter as methods of understanding and resistance outside the usual confines of rationality and respect (Ferrell, 1997). But anarchist criminology also incorporates a relatively complex critique of state law and legality which begins to explain why we might benefit from defying authority, or standing "against the law."

Many contemporary critical criminologists agree that state law as practiced in the United States is so thoroughly lubricated by economic privilege, intertwined with patriarchal arrangements, and protected by racist procedures as to constitute a mailed fist regularly brought down on the heads of women, the poor, ethnic minorities, young people, and other outsiders to economic power or state authority. Anarchist criminologists agree as well, but go on to argue that the practice of centralized state law harms people, groups, and the social fabric which joins them even if not aimed directly at "the powerless." Put differently, the administration of centralized state authority and legality destroys community, worsens criminality, and expands the abusive power of the state throughout the contemporary social order—and then, through its discriminatory practices, doubles this harm for those pushed to the bottom of this system. Among the broad harms of state legality:

1. State legality operates as what Pepinsky and Jesilow (1984) have called a "state-protection racket," extorting cash and conformity from those unlucky enough to be caught up in it. From speed traps to parking fines, from the plethora of licensing fees to the bureaucratized bungling of the IRS, the state operates as a vast revenue machine, an elaborate extortion device serving itself and those who operate it. And, as in any extortion operation or protection racket, state law provides for a host of state-sanctioned strong-arm tactics to enforce and enrich the fleece: impoundment, seizure, imprisonment, death. Clearly, such a system exists to perpetuate itself and to protect the powerful in and around it; the ideology that all of this occurs "in the interest of the community" seems at best a sort of cruel joke, or, to paraphrase the Wobblies, a cheap cologne sprinkled on the dunghills of state extortion. If you think otherwise, if you believe that this gigantic machine functions for us all, you might ask some frustrated middle class car owner trying to protest a parking ticket, some kid bankrupted and imprisoned for marijuana possession—or damn near any homeboy walking an inner city street.
2. Like a tangle of poisonous weeds, the labyrinth of state legality grows in the absence of human community, and once in place, further chokes possibilities for fluid and engaged human interaction. In a social world

increasingly fractured by alienated labor and economic inequality, privatized leisure, and the paranoia of the lonely crowd, police calls and civil suits proliferate—as does the sense that such disjointed, externalized tactics somehow constitute appropriate measures for solving disputes and achieving justice. But as parents file for (and are granted) restraining orders against three-year-old playground bullies (Thompson, 1996), as suits and countersuits multiply, as the daily fear of crime is shadowed by a daily fear of legal intrusion, human communities continue to unravel. Ultimately, a reliance on state legality reinforces the power and authority of centralized control systems, disables the potential for human community and human justice outside their bounds, and increasingly reduces human interaction to a stale dichotomy of legality and illegality.

3. As the interactionist/labeling tradition in criminology has taught us, the confinement of people and groups within state-administered categories of criminality, and within state-administered systems of punishment and retribution, promotes not rehabilitative humanity but rather a downward spiral of crime, criminalization, and inhumanity. For the individuals and groups targeted by such a system, the spiral intertwines disassociation from non-criminal communities, constricted personal and professional identities, growing anger and resentment, and finally an amplification of criminality and criminal careers. For the larger society, this spiral interweaves state and media sponsored fears of crime, an ideology of state-sanctioned retaliation, and thus broad paroxysms of objectification, dehumanization, and legal retribution. In this way, a system of state law and state "justice" perpetuates, within individual lives and larger social relations, the very problems it claims, falsely, to solve.
4. Within this system, the "rule of law" continues to proliferate, to penetrate more and more corners of social and cultural life (Cohen, 1979). As in a Weberian nightmare, state legality constitutes a sort of bureaucratic cancer that grows on itself, that produces an ever-expanding maze of legal control, and that in turn generates an ever-expanding body of bureaucratic and legal sycophants employed to obfuscate and interpret it. In 1886, Kropotkin (1975) documented "a race of lawmakers legislating without knowing what their laws are about ....legislating at random in all directions;" a century later, that race continues to spew forth legal regulation at a remarkable rate. As such legal controls grow in number and coverage, they of course constipate the conduct of social life, forcing all of us into ongoing contortions within and around them. More troubling, the proliferation of legal controls

finally suspends what little protection law once may have afforded. When every facet of social and cultural life is defined by legal control, and thus by state definitions of legality and illegality, we all remain continually vulnerable to the egregious exercise of state power. So, in a typical example, a recent series of highway drug busts in Arizona were predicated on a single traffic offense by drivers: "unsafe lane usage" (Steller, 1996). Finally, as state legality expands, we're all guilty—if not of "unsafe lane usage," then of another among the growing multitude of offenses. And finally, as the modern state and its many subdivisions make more and more of social and cultural life against the law, we must choose to stand against the law as well.

Against the Law: A Note on the Situated Politics of Crime and Resistance

Anarchist criminology's profoundly radical critique of state law as a system of inherent inhumanity, and its sense of therefore standing "against the law," leads to a criminology of crime and resistance as well. Labor historians and sociologists of work have long documented the pattern by which systems of authoritarian, alienating work generate among workers incidents of sabotage—of intentional rule-breaking and disruption—as a means of resisting these systems and regaining some sense of humanity and control. Anarchist criminologists suggest that this pattern may likewise be found in the interplay of state legal control and criminality. Rather than dismissing criminality as mindless misbehavior, or worse, simply accepting the state's construction of legality and illegality as definitive of good and bad human conduct, anarchist criminologists seek to explore the situated politics of crime and criminality. Put more simply, anarchist criminologists argue that the political (and politically inequitable) nature of state law and state criminalization means that acts of crime under such a system must also carry some degree of political meaning. And so, as with Foucault and Genet (Simon, 1991), anarchist criminologists seek to blur and explore the boundaries between crime and political resistance. This exploration neither assumes a priori that all crime constitutes resistance to state authority, nor ignores the often (but not always) negative consequences of criminality for people and communities. It does, though, call for paying careful attention to various criminal(ized) activities—graffiti writing, "obscene" art and music performances, pirate radio broadcasts, illegal labor strikes, curfew violations, shoplifting, drug use, street cruising, gangbanging, computer hacking (Ferrell 1995a, 1996; Ferrell & Sanders, 1995)—as a means of investigating the variety of ways in which criminal or criminalized behaviors may incorporate repressed dimensions of human dignity and self-determination, and lived resistance to the authority of state law.

Anarchist Criminology and Anarchist Community

As implied in its critique of centralized state authority, and its embracing of various alternatives to it, anarchist criminology calls for human communities which are decentralized, fluid, eclectic, and inclusive. Moreover, anarchist criminology proposes that this sense of inclusive, non-authoritarian community can benefit critical criminology itself. Clearly, anarchist criminology shares much with the epistemic uncertainty and situated politics of feminist criminology; with the decentered authority and textual deconstruction of postmodern and constitutive criminologies; with the critical pacifism of peacemaking criminology; and of course with the broader critique of legal injustice common to all critical criminologies. Even left realist criminology, though coming in some sense from a "direction polar opposite" (Einstadter & Henry, 1995) to that of anarchist criminology, shares with anarchist criminology a concern with identifying and exploring the situated consequences of crime and crime control. In the spirit of eclectic inclusivity, then, anarchist criminology argues against partitioning critical criminology into a series of small intellectual cubicles, and then closing one critical cubicle to the occupants of another (Pepinsky, 1991). Instead, anarchist criminology calls for an ongoing critical conversation among perspectives, for a multi-faceted critique of legal injustice made all the more powerful by its openness to alternatives. Cohen (1988) speaks of his "lack of commitment to any master plan (such as liberalism, left realism, or abolitionism), a failing, I would like to think, not of my own psyche but of the social world's refusal to correspond to any one theory." Anarchist criminology shares this lack of commitment to master plans—including its own—and embraces instead fluid communities of uncertainty and critique.

A Footnote on Failure

Perhaps an anarchist criminology, and an anarchist vision of justice or community, won't ultimately work. Perhaps, in its "pure" form—whatever "pure" might mean to an approach which embraces particularity, confusion, and adulteration—anarchism incorporates too much fluidity and disorder to ever construct itself fully. And perhaps so with anarchist criminology: as an approach which acknowledges no set boundaries, which claims no pedigreed intellectual heritage or exclusive scholarly turf, anarchist criminology may ultimately constitute no more than a defiant sensibility, an outlaw orientation and analysis, which floats around and against criminology (Cohen, 1988). From an anarchist viewpoint, of course, so much the better; for anarchists, nothing succeeds like uncertainty, nothing fails like success. And from this viewpoint, an anarchist criminology which fails to reach full fruition, which fails (and refuses) to "win out" over other perspectives, remains for this very reason an important thread in the larger project of critical criminology. For in a criminal justice universe of centralized and constricting authority, in an academic universe still largely fouled by mythologized standards of truth and imposed hierarchies of credibility (Becker, 1967), anarchist criminology functions if nothing else as a useful corrective to encrusted certainty and the desire for domination. And in this way, it undermines the tendency to embrace our own intellectual authority, or the exterior authority of the state, as appropriate—or worse, inevitable—frameworks for social order and social change.

In the 1600s British poet John Milton (1958), in his "Sonnet on His Blindness," reminded us that "they also serve who only stand and wait." Three hundred years later, the new wave of British film makers sharpened this notion's anarchic edge. In the film The Loneliness of the Long Distance Runner (Richardson & Sillitoe, 1962), lead character Colin Smith has been packed off to the harsh controls of the reformatory, where the headmaster manipulates him into running an importance race against a rival school. By the last few yards, Smith has the race won—and with it, approval of the headmaster, glory for the reformatory, and most importantly his own release from its confines. But just short of the finish line, Smith stops. While the rival school's runner passes him to win the race, Smith stands, stares, and smiles straight at the headmaster. And in his stopping, in his willful failure, he undermines his own hope for freedom—but at the same time undermines the labyrinth of rules and regulations, the daily degradations of obsequiousness and obedience, the phony ideologies of competitive loyalty to the institution and the state, through which his freedom and that of others has long been bought and sold.

So it is with anarchist criminology. Complete or incomplete, as intellectual critique or failed moment of visceral defiance, anarchist criminology serves if only by standing outside the law, by stopping short of the seductive ideologies of obedience and conformity which undergird it. And in this stance, in this disavowal of legal authority and it destructive effects on social and cultural life, anarchist criminology serves to remind us that human relations and human diversity matter—and that, in every case, they matter more than the turgid authority of regulation and law.

Author's Note

I thank Mark Hamm for ideas, inspiration, and the Dylan quote; and Harry Lyrico, who by word, deed and art, and despite his claims to the contrary, sketches the dangerous and honest beauty of life outside the boundaries of legality and privilege.

References

Bakunin, Michael. (1974). *Selected Writings.* New York: Grove Press.

Becker, Howard S. (1967). "Whose Side Are We On?" *Social Problems* 14: 239–247.

Cohen, Stanley. (1979). "The Punitive City: Notes on the Dispersal of Social Control." *Contemporary Crises* 3: 339–363.

Cohen, Stanley. (1988). *Against Criminology.* New Brunswick, NJ: Transaction.

DiCristina, Bruce. 1995. *Method in Criminology: A Philosophical Primer.* New York: Harrow and Heston.

Einstadter, Werner and Stuart Henry. (1995). *Criminological Theory: An Analysis of Its Underlying Assumptions.* Fort Worth, TX: Harcourt Brace.

Ferrell, Jeff. (1991). "The Brotherhood of Timber Workers and the Culture of Conflict." *Journal of Folklore Research* 28: 163–177.

Ferrell, Jeff. (1994). "Confronting the Agenda of Authority: Critical Criminology, Anarchism, and Urban Graffiti." In Gregg Barak, ed., *Varieties of Criminology: Readings from a Dynamic Discipline*, pages 161–178. Westport, CT: Praeger.

Ferrell, Jeff. (1995a). "Urban Graffiti: Crime, Control, and Resistance." *Youth and Society* 27: 73–92.

Ferrell, Jeff. (1995b). "Anarchy Against the Discipline." *Journal of Criminal Justice and Popular Culture* 3: 86–91.

Ferrell, Jeff. (1996). *Crimes of Style: Urban Graffiti and the Politics of Criminality.* Boston, MA: Northeastern.

Ferrell, Jeff. (1997). "Criminological Verstehen: Inside the Immediacy of Crime." *Justice Quarterly* 14: 3–23.

Ferrell, Jeff and Kevin Ryan. (1985). "The Brotherhood of Timber Workers and the Southern Lumber Trust: Legal Repression and Worker Response." *Radical America* 19: 55–74.

Ferrell, Jeff and Clinton R. Sanders (eds.). (1995). *Cultural Criminology.* Boston, MA: Northeastern.

Feyerabend, Paul. (1975). *Against Method.* London: Verso.

Godwin, William. (1971). *Enquiry Concerning Political Justice.* London: Oxford.

Goldman, Emma. (1969). *Anarchism and Other Essays.* New York: Dover.

Guerin, Daniel. (1970). *Anarchism.* New York: Monthly Review.

Industrial Worker. (1912). (Editorial). Spokane, WA: IWW. October 24: 2.

Industrial Worker. (1913). (Editorial). Spokane, WA: IWW. June 26: 2.

Kornbluh, Joyce (ed.). (1988). *Rebel Voices: An IWW Anthology.* Chicago: Charles H. Kerr.

Kropotkin, Peter. (1975). *The Essential Kropotkin.* New York: Liveright.

Marcus, Greil. (1989). *Lipstick Traces: A Secret History of the Twentieth Century.* Cambridge, MA: Harvard.

Mazor, Lester J. (1978). "Disrespect for Law." In Roland J. Pennock and John W. Chapman, eds., *Anarchism*, pages 143–159. New York: NYU.

Milton, John. (1958). "Sonnet on His Blindness." In Roy J. Cook, ed., *One Hundred and One Famous Poems*, page 91. Chicago: Reilly and Lee.

Ongerth, Steve and Radio Free Berkeley. (1995). "Challenging the Manufacture of Consent." *Z Magazine* 8: 18–22.

Pennock, Roland J. and John W. Chapman (eds.). (1978). *Anarchism.* New York: NYU.

Pepinsky, Harold E. (1978). "Communist Anarchism as an Alternative to the Rule of Criminal Law." *Contemporary Crises* 2: 315–327.

Pepinsky, Harold E. (1991). "Peacemaking in Criminology." In Brian D. MacLean and Dragan Milovanovic, eds., *New Directions in Critical Criminology*, pages 107–110. Vancouver: The Collective Press.

Pepinsky, Harold E. and Paul Jesilow. (1984). *Myths That Cause Crime*, 2nd ed. Cabin John, MD: Seven Locks.

Pepinsky, Harold E. and Richard Quinney (eds.). (1991). *Criminology as Peacemaking.* Bloomington: Indiana University Press.

Richardson, Tony (dir.) and Alan Sillitoe (screenwriter). (1962). *The Loneliness of the Long Distance Runner.* Great Britain: Woodfall Film Productions.

Ryan, Kevin and Jeff Ferrell. (1986). "Knowledge, Power, and the Process of Justice." *Crime and Social Justice* 25: 178–195.

Simon, John K. (1991). "Michel Foucault on Attica: An Interview." *Social Justice* 18: 26–34.

Steller, Tim. (1996). "Busted." *Arizona Daily Sun.* March 24: 1, 4, 5.

Stirner, Max. (1971). *The Ego and His Own.* New York: Harper and Row.

Thompson, Carolyn. (1996). "Sandbox 'Bully,' 3, Hauled into Court." *The Arizona Republic.* March 8: A1, A22.

Tifft, Larry. (1979). "The Coming Redefinition of Crime: An Anarchist Perspective." *Social Problems* 26: 392–402.

Tifft, Larry and Dennis Sullivan. (1980). *The Struggle to be Human: Crime, Criminology, and Anarchism.* Orkney: Cienfeugos.

2. *Communist Anarchism as an Alternative to the Rule of Criminal Law*[1]

HAROLD E. PEPINSKY

The rule of law (or deterrence of crime by law) and communist anarchism are symbiotic. Progress toward one will only be made in conjunction with progress toward the other. The logic of the rule of criminal law is so straightforward. It seems that it ought to work. Never mind the extended, recent arguments of American theorists like Van den Haag (1975) and Wilson (1975). Beccaria's (1968) short book, first published in 1764, makes the case neatly and compellingly. Make criminal law penalties just severe enough, and apply them swiftly and surely, and practically everyone should be deterred from committing any crime at all. If Americans in particular are inflicted with the disease of rising crime rates, and if there is no indication that imprisonment acts as a cure (Von Hirsch 1916), the fault lies not with the theory of law-imposed deterrence, but with a flawed application of the theory. Americans are simply not devoting sufficient resources to making imposition of the sanctions swift and sure.

Some argue that Beccaria logic itself is flawed, in that crime is really caused by class oppression, of which the rule of law is but an instrument.[2] If law can be seen as a cause at all, law causes, not prevents, crime, by defending the injustice of private ownership. Those holding this position do so as fallaciously as would the proponent of the view that blood pressure cannot be controlled by bio-feedback because blood pressure is in reality controlled by the autonomic nervous system. Even if class oppression is granted to be a cause of crime, and if one grants the moral argument that the real harm is done by the oppressors rather than by those treated as criminals, there is still no reason to question the logic that the all-powerful oppressors can keep the oppressed people from violating the terms of the law by applying the law swiftly, surely and severely enough. One can posit that the spirit of oppressed people is indomitable, but the proponents of Beccarian logic need only respond that this remains to be seen, just as it remains to be seen whether class oppression can be transcended.

Indiana University, Bloomington, IN, U.S.A.

On the other hand, Beccaria's logic is no refutation of the neat, compelling logic—preeminently of Berkman (1929)—that to eliminate government and its laws, and to permit people to partake of goods and services regardless of what they do in return, would also largely eliminate the injuries people do to one another—currently known as crimes. Communist anarchism is, even in theory, no easier to perfect than the rule of law, but the logic of communist anarchism has no more been impeached by proponents of the rule of law than have proponents of communist anarchism impeached the logic of the rule of law. And yet, in part no doubt because the two strategies are diametrically opposed means to the end (among others) of preventing crime, proponents of each side are viscerally opposed to one another.

Their opposition to one another is ill considered. Progress toward the rule of criminal law and progress toward communist anarchism are symbiotic. One will not happen without the other. The failure of each set of proponents to support the success of its counterpart strategy of crime control is an impediment to its own success. The partisans of the rule of criminal law and of communist anarchism are locked in a mixed-sum not a zero-sum game. Analyzing the issue in the American context, this essay is directed to showing that it behooves legalists and communist anarchists to cooperate with one another to achieve progress in crime control.

More Means Less: The Paradox of Perfecting the Rule of Criminal Law Throughout the United States, as this essay is written, Americans are caught up in the latest flood of attempts to perfect the rule of criminal law. The watershed from which these attempts flow is a decade old: the report of the President's Commission on Law Enforcement and Criminal Justice (1967), a grand attempt—as an element of building the Great Society—to set the agenda for American crime control. Since then, scholars and researchers have set about helping localities, states and the federal government make application of the law swift, sure and severe enough to deter crime. Criminal and juvenile codes have been revised in many states. Not to be out-done, the federal government first enacted the Omnibus (imagine!) Crime Control and Safe Streets Act in 1968, and now appears to be on the verge of enacting a comprehensive recodification of federal criminal law. Educational and training standards for all manner of criminal justice functionaries have been increased. New programs have proliferated to fill gaps in the old. Personnel and hardware (and now even software) have been added to make application of the law swifter and surer. Systems analysts and social science evaluators have been employed to rationalize criminal justice operations. The federal government, especially through the agency of the Law Enforcement Assistance Administration, has lavished funds on finding and attempting to solve problems of perfecting the rule of criminal law. State and regional planning agencies have been established to apply these funds. Together with their federal counterparts, the state and regional planning agencies have in most cases made religious use of the scriptures from the latest Presidential commission: the National Advisory Commission on Criminal Justice Standards and Goals (1973). Recent scholarly reinventions of Beccarian logic have gained tremendous popularity.

For all this effort, crime rates have in general continued to increase, if anything faster than ever. So glaring has the failure been to make application of American criminal law swift, sure and severe enough to deter crime, that (again as this essay is written) even the Law Enforcement Assistance Administration is rumored to be on the brink of an ignominious demise. All this occurs just as victim data are becoming regularly available, which show the amount of crime in need of criminal justice management to be as much as ten times as great as had been revealed in police data.

The faster Americans go in trying to perfect the rule of criminal law, the more behind they get. Why? The rule of criminal law will fail for want of any of its three elements: swiftness, sureness or severity. Imagine each of these elements to be the south pole of a magnet, and imagine further the problem of perfecting the rule of criminal law to be like the problem of drawing these poles of all three magnets together, and you have a fair approximation of the paradox of the rule of criminal law. Strengthen the field of any of the magnets, and it will repel the others further than ever. Make criminal justice functionaries apply the law more swiftly, and the capacity to apply the law surely (without error) to every crime will grow more remote. The more severe the sanction to be imposed, the greater the complexity of review of that imposition—the American extremes being the summary imposition of traffic fines and the elaborate trial and appellate procedures for review in capital cases. The more complex the review of the imposition of a sanction, the longer the delay in imposing the sanction. It has repeatedly been found that raising sanctions lowers the propensity of officials to arrest and prosecute (as happened following enactment of the "Rockefeller drug law" mandating life sentences for drug sale in New York State [*New York Times*, 1976]), while lowering the severity of penalties makes arrest and prosecution surer (as happened following the reduction of statutory penalties for marihuana possession in Nebraska [Galliher, McCartney and Baum 1974]). Ross (1976) and Wilson (1975), too, find an inverse relation between sureness and severity. Swiftness, sureness and severity are mutually exclusive.

If the magnets are to rest closer to each other, their fields must be weakened. Similarly, if the rule of criminal law is to be approached, the force with which swiftness, sureness and severity of imposition of criminal sanctions is pursued must be reduced. This is reflected in experimental and quasi-experimental findings on deterrence. It is where the severity of sanctions is lowest, in traffic law, that sporadic campaigns of swift, sure enforcement have been found to have temporary deterrent effects on parking and moving violations. The campaigns are bound to be sporadic, and the effects only temporary, because swift and sure enforcement cannot be routinely sustained. The magnet analog: weaken the field on one of the magnets to a bare minimum, suddenly push the magnets together, and you will succeed in bringing them close, but you will have trouble holding them long without somehow losing your grip. (As it happens, it has been found in research on learning that the magnitude of a reinforcer has much less to do with the rate of response than do the swiftness and sureness of reinforcement (Rachlin 1970). Beccaria himself emphasized the waste of making penalties more severe than minimally necessary, which in part contributed to his argument against capital punishment. Americans would do well to note that Scandinavian countries and the Netherlands appear to be doing relatively well at crime control with, by American standards, remarkably low-level sanctions.)

To sustain an approximation of the rule of criminal law, to sustain deterrence of crime, as in bringing the magnets closer by weakening their fields, the force with which law is applied must be reduced. In theory, in any community, the fewer the resources invested in applying the law to any form of behavior, the more effectively the rule of criminal law will operate to deter that behavior from occurring. Practically speaking, this means that the lower the rate—by population of the community—at which criminal justice agencies take jurisdiction over a kind of crime, the less likely it will be that that kind of crime will occur.

Note that this relationship is the same that would be predicted, but interpreted differently, by proponents of communist anarchism. As Berkman puts it:

> The truth is that what is called 'law and order' is really the worst disorder, as we have seen in previous chapters. What little order and peace we do have is due to the good common sense of the joint efforts of the people, mostly in spite of the government ... the interference of any government or authority can only hinder their efforts. (1929)

Is the bottle half empty or half full? Whether one concludes that the most effective deterrent is the one that needs invoking least, or that if people get along it is because they are left alone, the result is the same. In either case, the criminal justice system works best where it works least.

This is consistent with the findings of a number of recent studies, notably those conducted by American economists, interpreted to indicate that severer and surer criminal sanctions deter crime more (Palmer 1977). Literally, the findings are that the more rarely the criminal justice system takes jurisdiction over an offense, i.e. the more rarely an offense appears in police offense reports or in arrest figures, the likelier and severer the sanctions imposed for that offense will be. This is interpreted to indicate that sure, severe sanctions reduce the likelihood of crime. Now it also happens generally that the more rarely officials report an offense, the more serious the offense is in the eyes of the community. At extremes, disorderly conduct is commonly reported and regarded as a trivial offense, while assassinations of popular political figures and multiple murders are rarely reported and are (perhaps, in part, therefore) regarded as especially heinous. Restated, the findings of the so-called deterrence studies are intuitively obvious: community sentiment will most probably support successful prosecution of crimes and imposition of heavy sanctions in the relatively rare instances in which the criminal justice system is mobilized to respond to what, in that community, will be regarded as especially heinous crimes. That is, the criminal justice system responds most surely and severely to those forms of behavior that—for whatever reason—seldom occur and receive the weight of official attention. The government best deters those acts which people are least likely to commit in the first place. Or, the more rarely the law is applied to a form of behavior, the better it deters.

Thus, the findings of deterrence studies are consistent with the logic of the magnet analog to deterrence, which supports the communist anarchist premise that the less the government reacts to people's behavior, the better people behave. If perfection of the rule of criminal law is to be pursued with apparent success, it will only be as communities manage their affairs with less resort to criminal justice intervention. Those who would arrange for the law to be a stronger deterrent to crime had best help develop community mechanisms which disengage the communities from utilization of criminal justice services, lest the burden of crime control impede the swift, sure, severe application of the law.

I will return to a sketch of some ways in which a communist anarchist program for strengthening the rule of criminal law might be implemented. Meanwhile, let us consider the corollary argument that progress toward communist anarchism requires that criminal justice workers be made freer to perform their functions as they see fit.

The Ambiguous Status of the Communist Anarchist's Criminal Justice Worker

American governments employ a large and rapidly growing number of criminal justice workers. In 1971, the criminal justice labor force (National Criminal Justice Information and Statistics Service 1976) grew to more than one percent of the total American labor force, including nearly three million armed forces personnel (US Census 1974). The number of criminal justice workers passed the million mark in 1973 (National Criminal Justice Information and Statistics Service 1976). The total American labor force grew just over eight percent from 1970 to 1974 (US Census 1974), while the criminal justice labor force grew more than twenty-eight percent (US Census 1974). As of October 1975, there were reported to be 1,128,569 criminal justice employees in the country, of which 97,623 worked for the federal government, 274,319 worked for state governments, and 756,627 (half a million of them in law enforcement) for local governments (National Criminal Justice Information and Statistics Service 1977).

Criminal justice workers are becoming unionized and occasionally even striking for better pay and job conditions. Even grassroots criminal justice workers can wield considerable political power. About five years ago, a reformist commissioner of corrections was appointed, with strong words of gubernatorial endorsement, in the politically liberal State of Minnesota. The commissioner announced his intention to close down the reformatory in the town of St. Cloud. The community rose in anger; the community kept its reformatory and its members their jobs, while the commissioner resigned his. Criminal justice workers are a large, rapidly growing political force with which to be reckoned in planning crime control strategy.

Workers are the hero(in)es in the communist anarchist scenario. At the heart of the communist anarchist revolution is the workers' expropriation of the industries in which they work. "In expropriating, you stay on the job and you put the boss out. He may remain only on equal terms with the rest: a worker among workers" (Berkman 1929, 60). Berkman emphasizes the "constructive", nature of this aspect of the revolutionary process. Presumably, the workers continue producing, having now become their own bosses.

What if the product of the workers happens to be arrests, prosecutions, confining inmates or the like? Literally, as Berkman puts it, "anarchism means doing away with the state or government altogether" (1929, 11). The enigmatic position of government workers whose product is force or violence had presented itself by the time Berkman wrote (most of all in the case of professional soldiers in standing armies), but Berkman and (as far as I can see) every other communist anarchist writer has overlooked the problem. The writer who has come closest to addressing the matter is Godwin, first published in 1793:

> If juries might at length cease to decide, and be contented to invite, if force might gradually be withdrawn, and reason trusted alone, shall we not one day find, that juries themselves, and every other species of public institution, may be laid aside as unnecessary? Will not the reasonings of one wise man, be as effectual as those of twelve? Will not the competence of one individual to instruct his neighbours, be a matter of sufficient notoriety, without the formality of an election? (1971)

"At length," perhaps. For the time being, it would be difficult to get criminal justice workers out of the habit of giving orders, or to get citizens to interpret official invitations as devoid of coercion. There is no particular indication that the mass of criminal justice workers would readily be accepted as sages in their communities. Until communism were sufficiently perfected that former criminal justice workers could maintain decent standards of living without earning their pay, criminal justice officials who gave up coercion would be hard pressed to make their livelihood.

Suppose the problem were resolved in favor of trying to dispense with criminal justice workers. To get to know criminal justice workers—especially those in lower status occupations, e.g. police officers and prison guards rather than judges and prosecutors—is to find the view prevailing among them that a major effort is required to defend against this very treatment. Many criminal justice workers see themselves as engaged in a struggle against much of the citizenry for their professional survival. The defense is quite reasonable and fairly straightforward: organize, make oneself more desperately needed, and proliferate. Parkinson's Law aside[3] (Viano 1976), defense against attacks on their social standing encourages criminal justice workers to help swell their own ranks into a larger fighting force.

The most potent political weapon criminal justice workers have is the authority they are given to define the size of the crime problem they are called upon to manage. As long ago as 1858, the police in New York City discovered that if they made more arrests, they could show thereby that they had a bigger problem to manage and hence required an enlarged budget[4] (Villaume 1978). A little more than a century later, the same police force revised its offense reporting practices and arranged for the overall offense rate to increase 72 percent between 1965 and 1966 (Weinraub 1967). In the courts, case backlogs can be extended to support the call for increased resources. In prisons, complaints by inmates can serve as a basis for lobbying to enlarge facilities and staffs. Probation and parole revocation proceedings can be used as evidence that more personnel are needed to give greater attention to clients. Just as the species, like the rabbit, that are most heavily preyed upon breed the fastest, and as the human beings that are most destitute tend to reproduce at the highest rates in order to survive, so the species of worker—in criminal justice—that is especially heavily criticized proliferates in order to survive. Communist anarchists and others who seek to defeat the criminal justice system by attacking it defeat their own purposes instead, for the criminal justice bureaucracy expands in response.

The phenomenon is familiar. Bomb the British in London or the Vietnamese in Hanoi, and you have more British and more Vietnamese fighting for their cause with greater determination than ever. Try to take heroin away from those who depend on it, and the supply and demand for heroin is apt to increase. Communist anarchists in general and Berkman in particular are especially sensitive to the self-defeating character of com-pulsing. The fundamental principle of communist anarchism—that people who themselves are liberated from force and compulsion will be least likely to use force and compulsion against others—suggests that criminal justice workers will most readily give up their use of force when, instead of being attacked and threatened with loss of livelihood and community respect, they are entrusted with the management of their own pursuits and given respect and dignity.

There is some indication that the granting of respect can be effective in diverting criminal justice workers from acts of compulsion. It is a common feature of American traffic enforcement that a show of respect to a police officer is the best way for the motorist to avoid a traffic citation (Pepinsky 1976, 64–65). Criminal justice workers can—and do—rationalize that the respect they want—for their own sakes is the best indicator they can get that persons whom they meet in the course of their work are inclined to respect and follow the law itself. From the vantage point of the criminal justice worker, the better s/he is treated, and the less conflicts s/he encounters, the less serious "the crime problem" appears.

Part of the insecurity that criminal justice workers suffer is the threat of job curtailment or of salary increases insufficient to maintain current standards of living for him/herself or—more especially in many cases—for his/her dependents. If all criminal justice workers were given life tenure in the manner of federal judges and guaranteed that their incomes would minimally keep pace with the cost of living, they would not have reason to go to the trouble of drumming up more business and creating a pretext for public so port. There would be greater reluctance to authorize new positions in the criminal justice system if each involved a lifetime commitment to keep someone's standard of living safe against inflation, and so the growth of the criminal justice labor force would be further retarded. Life tenure with high enough pay increments would also serve to delay retirement of criminal justice workers. Younger police officers I rode with used to tell me what a problem it was that veteran officers stopped enforcing the law with vigor and enthusiasm. There is probably a general tendency for criminal justice workers, with age and experience, to become more jaded about their capacity to reform others. From the point of view of relieving the citizenry from compulsion and intervention, it would be so much the better if the criminal justice system grew to be composed mainly of easygoing service veterans. Such a work force would be especially amenable to helping turn its business back over to communities for their self-management.

Absent the threat of doing themselves out of jobs, the workers would respond to any extra pay incentive to reduce their caseloads, although this incentive would have to be kept low enough so that the capacity of private persons to manage their own affairs could keep pace with reduction in the force of crime control. Otherwise, the panic people suffered at being suddenly denied the criminal justice protection they had thought they had would set a self-fulfilling prophecy in motion: Fear of vulnerability to violence would promote exaggerated, violent acts of self-defense, against which people would have to defend themselves more forcefully than they had previously needed to do, and so on until—like Germans forty years ago—Americans panicked by the threat of social chaos welcomed a political order that promised control through terror if necessary.

Berkman recognizes the importance of the thrust of a communist anarchist social revolution's being "not destruction but construction" (Berkman 1929, 41). He argues that extensive preparation, particularly of workers learning to practice communist anarchist principles among themselves, is a necessary precondition of the social revolution he seeks (Berkman 1929, 50–62). In these days in the United States in which corporate ownership of the means of production of goods and services has so far replaced private ownership and in which the middle class is so preponderant now that the distinction between workers and owners has become blurred, one wonders how preparation for the sudden, dramatic social revolution could proceed far enough for the revolution to succeed unless success had already been achieved by the preparation itself. For the time being, at least, the insecurity of people inside and outside the criminal justice system needs to be recognized and attended to. The increased security that leads criminal justice workers to give up their use of force must lead them to do so gradually, or the insecurity of the citizenry will reproduce backlash that will eventually make government more tyrannical than ever. In the interest of progress toward communist anarchism, respect must be afforded the security and protection symbolized by criminal justice workers.

"Let's Be Realistic," or "Optimization in Defense of Idealism Is No Vice"

It is a tribute to the abiding optimism of Americans that so many of them can respond to their mounting crime problem with such naive romanticism. Were Berkman alive today, he might well be encouraged by the failure of Americans to be discouraged into nihilism by the growing levels of violence and predation they suffer at one another's hands. Instead, many Americans confidently proclaim that an ideal that has never come close to being achieved in practice can indeed be attained—deterrence of crime by perfection of the rule of law.

Communist anarchists are themselves often accused of naive romanticism for believing that what has at most been achieved for short periods in small communities could be achieved enduringly in large societies. They, too, should be commended for their enduring optimism. But to be practical, proponents of the rule of law and of communist anarchism should recognize that as purists, rejecting one another's positions out of hand, they only make their own ideals more elusive than ever. If the rule of law is ever to move from fantasy into practice, people must learn to get along without government. If communist anarchism is ever to move from fantasy into practice, people must give dignity and respect to those who work to serve them in their government. Rule-of-law and communist anarchist proponents make progress together or not at all. Although on their face the establishment of the rule of criminal law and the abolition of government protection of rights (basically of property holdings and entitlements) are antithetical, the strategy that optimizes progress toward both objectives also maximizes progress toward each.

The basic principle upon which the mutual progress toward the rule of law and communist anarchism rests is simple: regardless of whether people in society happen to work in government, if they have the courage to trust, respect and dignify one another for their ability to get along together fairly, the prophecy will tend to fulfill itself, while if people act out of fear and distrust for one another, their fears will be realized instead. At the societal level, as manifested in the growth of crime, and at the individual level, as manifested in what Lemert (1962) describes as "paranoia and the dynamics of exclusion," the course of distrust and fear is all too familiar to Americans. Given Americans' history, interpersonal fear and distrust are established both "empirically" and "objectively" for them, regardless of ideological persuasion. Practically all Americans share the view that progress requires that some personal enemy be destroyed. Whether their particular enemy happens to be anarchists, capitalists, communists, conservatives, criminals, jews, liberals, hippies, Indians, mafiosi, men, Nixon, owners, politicians, rednecks, rulers, or others, Americans are remarkably united in the wisdom—yea, even the necessity—of pursuing a self-defeating strategy to achieve social harmony: "they" must be subjugated by whatever weapons (the grander the better) that "we" may develop.

If Americans are to make progress toward crime control, they must learn to subjugate their own distrust not that of other people, and empower those they now fear to act fearlessly. This is no more or less practicable than is progress either toward the rule of law or toward communist anarchism. If American criminal justice workers, whose job currently is to distrust the citizenry, cannot afford to trust and empower them instead, and if the citizenry cannot afford to trust and empower their criminal justice workers, then they deceive themselves by believing that either the rule of law or communist anarchism is approachable.

Except for tenure and guaranteed pay increments for criminal justice workers, a set of concrete proposals for optimizing deterrence and anarchism appears elsewhere (Pepinsky 1976, 119–132). Besides tenure with assured cost-of-living pay increases, it is proposed that criminal justice workers be given bonuses for not filing official reports of any kind (not just selected reports as was done with police in Orange, California [Greiner 1974]). To encourage private settlement of disputes without resort to official arbitration, it is proposed that state mediation services be established, which would be forbidden (a) to set conditions on initiation or termination of client contact, (b) to keep files of otherwise unavailable information, (c) to act as legal representatives for clients, or (d) to take any action on clients' behalf outside of their physical presence, lest the mediation tum into another form of arbitration. I would add that mediation workers could be given pay bonuses for declines in arrest rates (which would signify reduced entry of cases into the criminal justice process).

To encourage the private sector of the community to stabilize its relations, thereby having less occasion to resort to government intervention in people's affairs, it is proposed that a tax/subsidy mechanism be established to encourage employers to profit most by decreasing class disparities in their society. Employers would qualify for the subsidy by simultaneously employing more full-time workers and raising the income of their lowest paid full-time workers faster than the rate of inflation. Otherwise, they would be taxed. This would reward and dignify employers for making progress toward communism, while increasing the respect, dignity and material welfare of workers. The challenge of optimizing progress toward the rule of law and communist anarchism is to empower and dignify all citizens equally, whether they work in or out of government, and whether or not they manage production. In place of the impotence Americans now feel that tends to make everyone believe that the solution of social problems must be someone else's responsibility, everyone must be made freer to take her/his social position and survival for granted as s/he helps and allows others to pursue their own interests more freely.

Whether, as proponents of the rule of law, they look to written standards of fair exchange for their salvation, or as proponents of communist anarchism, they look instead to the obsolescence of standards of exchange, Americans are misled by assuming a dualism between what Kalven and Zeisel (1966, 8) refer to as a government of law and a government of men. The two are symbiotic. Law rules more the less it is imposed, and law is imposed less the more its agents are respected. Were the rule of law to become absolute, people would have ceased reckoning the equation of value given and value received among themselves, as deterrence perfected made referral to formal standards of exchange obsolete.

Proponents of the rule of law and of communist anarchism are equally correct in their diagnosis: the growth of crime reflects both a failure of deterrence and a failure to leave people free to tend their own affairs. On the other hand, the treatment prescribed by both sides is equally wrong, for increasing the force of criminal justice and generating resistance to criminal justice workers both promote crime. Americans would do well to accept the twin diagnoses and have confidence in the promise underlying two romantic and as yet remote visions of how to control crime. If Americans have enough faith in deterrence to help people to act without government intervention, and enough faith in freedom from government compulsion to give dignity to government workers, crime will become less of a problem for them.

Notes

1. This was to be a revision of a paper, "Anarchist-Communism as an Alternative to Due Process," delivered at the Society for the Study of Social Problems Meeting, New York, 1976. As it turns out, the spirit is the same but the content is entirely different. Special thanks for criticism through versions of both papers go to Jill Bystydzienski, Drew Humphries, John Laub, Barton Parks, Pauline Pepinsky, Vic Streib, an anonymous anarchist in New York City, and from *Contemporary Crises*, Bill Chambliss and anonymous reviewers. Special thanks for typing this and the remainder of the pile I have recently laid on, go to Martha Geter and Donna Littrell.
2. As, for instance, has R. Quinney (1974).
3. Costello (1885), as reported in Inciardi (1976), in Viano (1976, 179–180).
4. In "Parkinson's Law and the United States Bureau of Prisons," Alfred Villaume (1978) makes the case that Parkinson's Law operates in the federal corrections bureaucracy, as it probably operates elsewhere.

References

Beccaria, C. 1968. (H. Paolucci, trans.) *On Crimes and Punishments.* Indianapolis, IN: Bobbs-Merrill.

Berkman, A. 1971, originally published in 1929. *ABC of Anarchism.* London: Freedom Press.

Costello, A. E. 1885. *Our Police Protectors: History of the New York Police from the Earliest Period to the Present Time.* New York: author's edition.

Galliher, J. F., J. L. McCartney and B. Baum. 1974. "Nebraska's Marihuana Law: A Case of Unexpected Legislative Innovation." *Law and Society Review*, 8: 441–455.

Godwin, W. 1971. "Enquiry Concerning Political Justice." In S. Schatz (ed.), *The Essential Works of Anarchism*, pp. 3–41. New York: Bantam Books.

Greiner, J. M. 1974. *Tying City Pay to Performance: Early Reports on Orange, California, and Flint, Michigan.* Washington, DC: Labor-Management Relations Service of the National League of Cities, National Association of Counties, United States Conference of Mayors.

Kalven, H., Jr., and H. Zeisel. 1966. *The American Jury.* Boston, MA: Little, Brown & Co.

Lemert, E. M. 1962. "Paranoia and the Dynamics of Exclusion." *Sociometry* 25 (March): 2–25.

National Advisory Commission on Criminal Justice Standards and Goals. 1973. *Courts, Corrections, Police (3 reports).* Washington, DC: United States Government Printing Office.

National Criminal Justice Information and Statistics Service. 1976. *Trends in Expenditure and Employment Data for the Criminal Justice System: 1971–1974.* Washington, DC: United States Government Printing Office, p. 18.

National Criminal Justice Information and Statistics Service. 1977. *Expenditure and Employment Data for the Criminal Justice System: 1975.* Washington, DC: United States Government Printing Office.

New York Times. September 5, 1976. "Study Backs Critics of New York Drug Law." (1, 40).

Palmer, J. 1977. "Economic Analyses of the Deterrent Effect of Punishment." *Journal of Research in Crime and Delinquency* 14: 2–4.

Pepinsky, H. E. 1976. *Crime and Conflict: A Study of Law and Society.* London: Martin Robertson and New York: Academic Press.

President's Commission on Law Enforcement and Administration of Justice. 1967. *The Challenge of Crime in a Free Society.* Washington, DC: United States Government Printing Office.

Quinney, R. 1974. *Critique of Legal Order: Crime Control in Capitalist Society.* Boston, MA: Little, Brown.

Rachlin, H. 1970. *Introduction to Modern Behaviorism.* San Francisco, CA: W. H. Freeman.

Ross, H. L. 1976. "The Neutralization of Severe Penalties: Some Traffic Law Studies." *Law and Society Review* 10: 403–413.

United States Bureau of the Census. 1974. *Statistical Abstract of the United States: 1974.* Washington, DC: United States Government Printing Office, p. 336.

Van den Haag, E. 1975. *Punishing Criminals: Concerning a Very Old and Painful Question.* New York: Basic Books.

Viano, E. 1976. *Victims and Society.* Washington, DC: Visage Press.

Villaume, A. C. 1978. "Parkinson's Law and the United States Bureau of Prisons." *Contemporary Crisis* 2(2): 209–214.

Von Hirsch, A. 1916. *Doing Justice: The Choice of Punishment.* New York: Hill and Wang.

Weinraub, B. 1967. "Crime Reports Up 72% Here in 1966: Actual Rise is 6.5%." *New York Times.* February 21.

Wilson, J. Q. 1975. *Thinking About Crime.* New York: Basic Books.

3. *Lombroso and the Anarchists: Anarchism in the Formation of Criminology*

Jeff Shantz

Cesare Lombroso, the dominant orthodox figure in the establishment of criminology as academic discipline, dedicated a great deal of his research, study, and writing to the analysis of anarchists, as prototypical agitators. The anarchists provide one of the primary resources for Lombroso's multisectional "Illustrative Studies in Criminal Anthropology." Indeed, Lombroso suggests that the study of the physiognomy of the political criminal provides perhaps the most practical application of Criminal Anthropology (capitalization in the original).

Lombroso's interests in anarchists as a significant criminal type emerge very early on in his work. He develops a lengthy discussion of the anarchist criminal figure in 1891 in his article "Illustrative Studies in Criminal Anthropology. III. The Physiognomy of the Anarchists" published in the journal The Monist, a publication produced by Edward C. Hegeler and recognized as one of the most significant journals in philosophy.

Such study of anarchists, as the prototypical political criminal, according to Lombroso, furnishes nothing less than the juridical basis of political crime, something which had seemed to elude earlier researchers and their research. Indeed, Lombroso suggests that before his research it was common for analysts and laypeople alike to conclude that there was no political crime. Certainly, that was the conclusion of jurists, Lombroso argues. Note that Lombroso does not address, or seem even to conceive of political crime as an activity of elite institutions, such as the government or criminal justice systems.

In a 1900 article, “A Paradoxical Anarchist,” published in Popular Science Monthly, Lombroso notes that up to that point much of his research on anarchists had been done only through indirect or secondhand studies. Those indirect studies involved analysis of data furnished by journals, legal proceedings, and handwriting analyses (!) of small numbers of anarchist subjects. He notes, for example, his attempts to study supposed anarchists Caserio and Luccheni through indirect means. Lombroso actually bemoans the fact that he has only rarely had the opportunity to examine a “real live” anarchist directly and “make those measurements and craniological determinations” without which study is reduced to an approximation and remains merely hypothetical (1900, n.p.). Yet none of this stopped him from making a range of rather extreme claims against anarchists based on no direct contact with any of his “subjects” and with only limited, often entirely inaccurate, information about the movements and groups they were said to be a part of.

At the same time, and despite this lack of meaningful information, anarchists posed a central and significant concern for Lombroso and, indeed, serve as significant targets for his research. One might suggest, in fact, that much of Lombroso’s criminological analysis is developed through a fascination with anarchism. Without the figure of the anarchist Lombroso’s work would surely have lacked spectacular effect and political influence, as well as social impact.

We might also mention that Lombroso’s work had an impact beyond criminology. Depictions of anarchism based on Lombroso’s work are used to spruce up portrayals of anarchists in Joseph Conrad’s The Secret Agent and G.K. Chesterton’s The Man who was Thursday.

The Physiognomy of the Anarchists

In his most developed physical analysis of anarchists, “The Physiognomy of the Anarchists” (1891), Lombroso asserts that the anarchists of Turin and Chicago, whose photographs provide the sole basis for his study, are often representative of what he terms the criminal type. Yet he is careful to clarify that this does not mean that they are “true criminals.” Rather, the anarchists possess what he identifies as the degenerative characteristics said to be common both to criminals and the insane (a term that he never problematizes). Moreover these traits are said by Lombroso to be hereditary. His “evidence” for this is taken in the fact that John Wilkes Booth’s (who was no anarchist) father was called Junius Brutus and he gave his son the name of a revolutionary Wilkes. Curious evidence to be sure.

More than this, though, Lombroso's research can supply, in his modest view, a method for distinguishing "true revolution" (which is fruitful and useful) from mere rebellion or utopia (which are always sterile in his opinion) (1891, 336). True revolutionists, for Lombroso, whether one is speaking about political or scientific revolutions, are always geniuses or saints and they display "a marvelously harmonious physiognomy" (1891, 336). In evidence of this Lombroso refers his readers to the philosophies he provides in his work "Delitto Politico." There are the supposedly "noble physiognomies" of such as Mazzini, Paoli, Fabrizi, and Garibaldi. Notably these are figures of elite and authoritarian bents.

Lombroso describes the apparently saintly visages as follows:

> Generally we see in them a very large forehead, a very bushy beard, and very large and soft eyes; sometimes we meet with the jaw much developed, but never hypertrophic; sometimes, finally, with paleness of the face (Mazzini, Brutus, Cassius); but these characteristics seldom accumulate in the same individual to the extent of constituting what I call the criminal type. (1891, 337)

This initial sense is conformed for Lombroso by his "scientific studies" reported in the article. These take the form of a proportional analysis of traits identified by Lombroso solely from photographs of people identified (not necessarily confirmed) as anarchists.

Of 321 Italian revolutionists (of the non-revolutionary, progressive, saintly type) the proportion of the "criminal type" was only 0.57% according to Lombroso's photo observation. Of 30 Nihilists (who were being executed by a supposedly non-criminal Russian state) 18 had a quite fine physiognomy, while 12 showed some "isolated anomalies." Only two presented the criminal type (1891, 337). This is only 6.8%.

Yet when Lombroso turns to activists of the French Revolution, such as Marat, he finds they all show some criminal type. Never mind that he could not directly study, interview, or interact with any of them.

Sadly, the criminal type frequently appears, according to Lombroso, among the Communards and the anarchists. He can tell this by looking at the photos of people who have already been revealed to him as Communards and anarchists (of whom many have been targeted by the state as criminals for political views or actions). In no case does he identify anarchists from random samples of human photos but no matter. In 50 photos of Communards he finds the criminal type in 12%. The insane type (undefined) makes up a stunning 10% among the Communards. Out of 41 Parisian anarchists Lombroso studied along with Bertillon at the office of the Paris police, the criminal type was found present in 31%.

Following the rebellion of May Day 1890, Lombroso was fortunate enough to gain access to the photos of 100 Turin anarchists. Not surprisingly he found the criminal type to be present in the proportion of 34%. Yet this was still less than the occurrence of 43% shown by 280 ordinary prisoners at Turin (it is not clear if any of these were undeclared, hidden, or silent anarchists).

In fine positivist fashion, Lombroso provides a nice table detailing the precise percentage of characteristics found in each category, anarchist and ordinary criminals.

Of the one hundred anarchists arrested, 30% had been arrested before. Fifty percent of the ordinary prisoners were recidivists. So fully 70% of the arrested Turin anarchists had not been arrested for any criminal acts. They were only arrested in that case for political protest. Yet they are identified and analyzed by Lombroso as criminals.

Not content to limit his studies there, however, Lombroso also studies photographs of forty-three Chicago anarchists provided to him by his esteemed colleague Dr. Carus of The Open Court Publishing Company. Reflecting the central interest of criminologists in anarchism, Carus had previously published Schaack's "Anarchy and the Anarchists" (1889). Among the photographs of the poor workers of Chicago Lombroso finds a similar occurrence of the criminal type to the presumed anarchists of Turin, around forty percent.

In some, the facial anomalies are clear and pronounced for the observant scientist. In Lombroso's words:

> Especially in Potowski, Sugar, and Micolanda I mark facial asymmetry, enormous jaws, developed frontal sinus, protruding ears; and the same (except the asymmetry) in Seveski and Novak. Fielden has a turned up nose and enormous jaws; Most has acrocephaly and facial asymmetry. (1891, 338)

Of course, as anyone today knows and recognizes there is nothing like a police mugshot to offer a flattering portrait capturing a person in their relaxed human fullness. Nick Nolte and Gary Busey come on down.

Lombroso finds in the Haymarket martyrs—those punished or killed by the state—a singular repeated anomaly—ears without lobes (here Shantz must admit to exhibiting the very same anomaly). Of course, Lombroso has to note that this characteristic is "very frequent in normal men as well" (1891, 338). Thus, its appearance among some anarchists means—oh wait—absolutely nothing. Lombroso goes on to report that the ears are also protruding in all but August Spies. The jaw is much developed in some, including Louis Lingg, Spies, Fischer, and Engel. Lombroso reports that all except Spies have a "fine and full" forehead, showing "great intelligence" (1891, 338).

Here, however, Lombroso is forced to make an equivocal remark presented well after the fact and only in a footnote. The footnote confesses that the portrait Lombroso used from Schaack's work Anarchy and Anarchists is, according to information later provided by General Trumbull in Chicago, not at all true to life. Thus Lombroso is forced to admit: "It would seem, then, that the features upon which my opinion is based do not exist" (1891, 338). Again he provides his knowingly false analysis anyway and only offers this tidbit in a footnote. Even still, undeterred he goes on:

> In the plates of the journal Der Vorbote we find a Mongolic cast of feature in Engel and Lingg, both of whom should have much of the degenerative characters, enormous jaw and zygoma, and Lingg oblique eyes. But these characters are much less apparent in the photographs that I received from The Monist and in which the jaw of Fischer even decreases. (1891, 338–339)

It is not even clear that the photographs are even of the people they are claimed to represent. There is no certainty that they have not been misidentified or names misapplied.

Poor Fielden "has a wild physiognomy, not without sensuality" (Lombroso 1891, 339). Parsons and Neebe appear noble but August Spies is, once again, morbid in physiognomy. Notably, though, this time the physiognomy accords with Spies autobiography which is supposedly "written with a fierce fanaticism (Lombroso 1891, 339). The writings or Parsons and Neebe are said to be "calm and reflective" though certainly enthusiastic (Lombroso 1891, 339).

Having made his claim for the importance of studying anarchists, Lombroso then turns attention to the biographies of the Haymarket Martyrs for more suggestive historical antecedents. Albert Parsons is said to have had a very religious mother and father (well it is right in the name is it not?). Even more:

> Indeed, the Parsons since 1600 had as a family taken part in all revolutionary movements. A Tompkin, a relation of his mother, had taken part in the battles of Brandywine and of Monmouth; a General Parsons was an officer in the Revolution of 1776, and a captain Parsons engaged in the battle of Bunker Hill. (1891, 339–340)

August Spies was supposedly born in a chateau celebrated in stories of feudal robberies. The father of Louis Lingg had a concussion suffered during his work as a laborer. Fielden's father had been a leading advocate for agricultural lands for workers as well as a founder of the "Consumers Cooperative Society." Lombroso shows, as he does on many occasions, his class bias in describing Fielden's father as a powerful orator despite his occupation as a "workman" (1891, 340).

The hereditary influence is also revealed for Lombroso in the numbers of anarchist brothers who have been criminalized. Among them he names the Spies, the Djeneks, the Fieldens, and the Lehms. Each set of siblings also had parents who died because "they were old or diseased" (1891, 340). That point would seem, to the uneducated layperson perhaps, self-evident. Few assessments say as much about Lombroso's analytical capacity and the predictive quality of his theories as this.

Lombroso responds to those critics who might suggest that rather than viewing these forebears as criminals or lunatics, one might more productively understand them as visionaries or geniuses who raised visionaries or geniuses. Bodendick is proclaimed insane by Lombroso despite the obvious genius of his poetry, which was published. He is said to be "a mattoid," full of cunning and mischief (1891, 340). In his work "L'Homme de Génie" Lombroso had claimed that genius is simply "nervous epilepsy" and "almost all of the sons of men of genius are lunatics, idiots, or criminals" (1891, 340). Again, no evidence is given for these obviously incredible assertions. Undeterred, this point is repeated by Lombroso in his later works, including "Anarchy and its Heroes" (1897).

In addition to the hereditary contributions noted above there are notable personality features detailed by Lombroso, though it is unclear how he derives these from photo analysis and he, good scientist, would surely not rely on hearsay and rumor. George Engel was supposedly enthusiastic and impressionable and Lousi Lingg was apparently talkative. That the unfortunate, and wrongly accused, Lingg would kill himself before the state could do so (and to deny it the opportunity), provides for Lombroso only a sure sign of his "moral insensibility" (1891, 340). Spies is accused of having a real hatred for the rich. This would not be overly surprising for a poor social reformer who had known bitter poverty and social exclusion. Indeed, much of Lombroso's assessment relates to acts that did not occur or which were only rumored. This would reach absurd levels in his later article, "A Paradoxical Anarchist" (1900), in which he makes huge assumptions about anarchists based on a lone figure who may not have even been an anarchist and who turned himself before carrying through a plot that may have existed only in his own imagination.

He suggests that anarchists admired thieves and brigands but offers no evidence. This claim, in fact, flies in the face of much of anarchist theory and is contradicted by much of anarchist movement history.

"Anarchy and Its Heroes" (1897)

Lombroso again takes up his physiognomic analysis of anarchists in "Anarchy and Its Heroes." There Lombroso suggests: "It suffices to take a look at the portraits I gave in my Crime Politique to see how much the anarchists and the rebels who are anarchists of the past, present the perfect type of criminal, like Kammerer, Steilmacher, Brady, Fitzharris" (1897, 2).

In "Anarchy and Its Heroes," Lombroso tells the reader that a view of anarchist portraits suggests readily the criminal type. He reports:

> A distinguished magistrate, M. Spingardi, who was kind enough to furnish me with numerous materials for this article, said to me: As far as I am concerned, I have never seen an anarchist who was not either crippled, a hunchback or whose face wasn't asymmetrical. (1897, 2)

Ravachol and Prady, to name two, are said to present "the perfect type of born criminal" and not only in their faces but in their supposed "hatred of the family" (1897, 3). Again, a social analysis, involving critique of the monogamous nuclear family, with cultural and political significance, is presented as a marker of criminality rather than an aspect of social analysis. It is placed, by Lombroso, on the same footing as hysteria or physical infirmity.

Yet, at the same time, in contrast to the criminal type some supposedly criminal anarchists show features that suggest a different character. Of the apostle of propaganda of the deed, Vaillant, Lombroso says: "In the first place I'd like to say that his physiognomy was not at all that of a criminal, except perhaps for his too large and widely spaced ears. But he was a hysteric" (1897, 3). Vaillant is described as being "unbalanced" but more than a born criminal he is identified by Lombroso as "a true passionate fanatic" (1897, 3). On the other hand, Vaillant is further said to be "of a gentle and timid character" (1897, 3). Of course, all of this is to reveal that humans, criminal or otherwise, are complex, multifaceted beings who cannot be reduced to this or that trait or feature. The main point here, though, is the great attention that Lombroso gives to anarchists in developing his pseudo theory of crime and criminality.

The dubious character of Lombroso's analysis is reflected in his concluding notice on Vaillant that his "hatreds are explained by heredity and misfortune" (1897, 3). So the explanation is both biological and social-historical, but Lombroso says nothing more about which is most salient or the possible interactions between factors (if any). He offers, then, no analysis at all. He does say with regard to heredity, though, that "his birth was owed to a half-guilty love and to degenerate parents" (1897, 3). Here again, then, his hereditary analysis is really a statement of Lombroso's own morals with regard to premarital sex and sexual freedoms.

Lombroso then proceeds to list some experiences of economic deprivation and poverty against which the unfortunate man waged a "futile struggle" (1897, 3). Lombroso notes that early experiences of poverty and exploitation in labor made of him a rebel. Again, for Lombroso, resistance against economic injustice is simply a mark of some deviance or other (criminality, insanity, immorality, etc.).

Vaillant had found himself in hard labor before he was even a teenager. As Lombroso describes other youthful experiences, without stopping to reflect that he is actually condemning systems of economic and judicial inequality and oppression:

> And it is thus that this unhappy child of fourteen wandered from city to city, arrested here for having begged for a morsel of bread, condemned there for having, on a day when he was dying of hunger, taken without paying a meal that was worth 90 centimes. He tried everything, without success. His boss in Choisy-le-Roi gave him 20 francs a week, for himself, his wife and his child. They lacked bread almost every day. The great mobility, the instability proper to hysterics, which he had demonstrated in his various métiers, he also brought to his convictions. (1897, 4)

Not surprisingly given this life history of direct experiences he became a socialist. Incredibly, Lombroso suggests that his mobility was not due to poverty, horrible working conditions, and unemployment but rather a case of "the instability proper to hysterics" (1897, 4). Among the "analyses" carried out on his subjects Lombroso refers to handwriting analysis. On Vaillant he notes: "The graphologist who examines his signature finds there vanity, prode, and energy as the dominant characteristics. The large 'T,' the rising writing, the enormous initials are a striking proof of this" (1897, 4).

A Paradoxical Anarchist

Lombroso is happy to report, finally, in the Popular Science Monthly article, "A Paradoxical Anarchist," that he had recently found an opportunity "to observe a real anarchist in person" (1900, n.p.). He reports being able to study the anarchist according to the usual methods of his clinic. Lombroso is pleased to relay that the results of his studies were singular in shedding light on "the dark world of these agitators" (1900, n.p.).

For Lombroso, the lives of anarchists are marked by what he refers to as "strange contradictions" (1900, n.p.). Lombroso identifies the anarchist subject in his study as a young man, who, rather than having committed any crime, had actually given himself up to police with a claim that he had received a letter from Italian anarchists asking him to kill the king while in Turin. Yet the postal authorities claimed to have delivered to him no letter, of this or any other kind. Rather incredibly, given the construction of the man as a criminal, he had actually surrendered to authorities and renounced the plot (for which there was no actual evidence but the man's statement), expressing no desire to commit regicide, and seeming to abhor the idea in any event.

Yet, as Lombroso reports: "There was no real basis of criminal intent, but our police put him in prison, and there I found him" (1900, n.p.). So the supposed anarchist subject is entirely dubious as either a criminal, an agitator, or an anarchist. There is little to suggest he was any of these.

Despite this inconvenient fact, Lombroso soldiers on, driven by the excitement of access to his first living "anarchist" subject. Having relayed the immediate background to the anarchist and the context for his involvement with authorities, Lombroso offers a physiognomic sketch of the unfortunate fellow. According to Lombroso:

> His physiognomy presented all the characteristics of the born criminal and of the foolhardy and sanguinary anarchist. He had flaring ears, premature and deep wrinkles, small, sinister eyes sunk back in their orbits, a hollowed flat nose, and small beard—in short, he presented an extraordinary resemblance to Ravachol, as may be seen from their portraits. (1900, n.p.)

Lombroso goes on to describe:

> The cranium was a little smaller than the normal, and the upper part of the skull was much rounded and deformed, with a cephalic index of 91—considerably more rounded than the head of Luccheni. The horizontal fold of the hand was of a type much like that of Ravachol. (1900, n.p.)

Here Lombroso is at great pains to reference, for dramatic popular effect no doubt, an infamous figure (certainly for the European bourgeoisie) of much popular notoriety who was widely known for having….

This is clearly an attempt to build a case of guilt by association—on the basis of a flimsy claim of surface resemblance. Ironically, the two portraits that Lombroso includes in his article, one of the poor subject and one of Ravachol, show minimal resemblance at all, mostly around hair. Tellingly, the closest resemblance between the two is represented in their (still dissimilar) moustaches.

Lombroso suggests, with some pleasure, that the biological study that gave rise to "A Paradoxical Anarchist," involving the unfortunate confessor, revealed, well beyond the second hand studies of Caserio and Luccheni, a number of what he describes as "singular anomalies" (1900, n.p.). For example, there was:

> a touch six times more obtuse than the normal—six millimeters on the right, five on the left; a remarkably blunt sensitiveness to pain and dull perception of location; an extraordinarily reduced visual field, particularly in the left eye; a somewhat tremulous handwriting, and slight defects of articulation in speech; and thin hair. (1900, n.p.)

While one might readily acknowledge these as effects of poverty and/or a life of hard work, Lombroso sees only traits of a criminality that is not even hinted at by the details of the case at hand. When turning to personality issues,

Lombroso is forced to concede that there is nothing striking in that regard at all. The reluctant anarchist spoke kindly of his parents and would have liked to see them. Apparently, though, he had "a blunt moral sense" though it is not clear how that was ascertained beyond the perception that he was an anarchist and that, in and of itself, automatically confirmed the diagnosis (in a very nicely circular fashion).

The young man had supposedly attempted suicide at 13 and had been in jail at 16. It was in jail on Brescia, apparently, that he claimed to have met 30 anarchists. This claim came despite the relevant authorities insisting that there were not 30 anarchists in the jail, a fact that could be readily confirmed.

Incredibly, Lombroso claims to have gotten to the bottom of the subject's ambiguous anarchy after observing the effects of a liter of wine, administered by the sage professor, on the prisoner. Under the influence of alcohol, as Lombroso records:

> [H]e began to exclaim, 'Viva l'anarchio!' (Hurrah for anarchy!), 'Morte al Re!' (Death to the king!), to kiss a dagger [supplied by whom is not said], to break various things against imaginary guards, and, after a short period of quiet, to swear and forswear himself that his companions had done what he had done, that they had shouted for anarchy, had broken the vases, and had desired to kill the king. (1900, n.p.)

Needing more scientific confirmation of this initial outcome of prescribed booze, Lombroso set up a little experiment for the unfortunate lad. Lombroso reports:

> I began by giving him ten, then twenty, then thirty, then forty grammes of alcohol, up to eighty. I observed that his personality began to change after forty grammes. He became somewhat insolent and suspicious, and had vague delirious imaginings of persecutions. When invited to sing anarchistic songs he refused, evidently fearing to compromise himself, but sang them voluntarily in an undertone. When the dose of alcohol was increased to ninety grammes his personality seemed immediately to undergo a full change; his touch became twice as fine (three millimetres), and his visual field increased threefold; he declared that there was a spy around. When put into his cell he sang anarchistic hymns, threatened death to the king, bandied a box as if brandishing a dagger, climbed to a window and insulted the sentinel, resisted five men who tried to disarm him, and continued in this condition for eight hours. (1900, n.p.)

The next day (with or without a hangover) the subject denied having committed any of the actions attributed to him and, even more, proclaimed himself "a good monarchist and a good citizen" (1900, n.p.). One might well ask, then, why the fellow was not identified and analyzed as a "paradoxical monarchist" or a "paradoxical citizen" and the degenerate traits of these social types detailed. Such is the character of Lombroso's "science" of criminology.

Lombroso's response was, in fact, to extend the "experiment." He relays:

> On renewing the experiment a few days afterward with eighty grammes of alcohol, the same series of phenomena recurred—a real anarchistic raving, a genuine mania for regicide, which would certainly have ended in some act if he had not been restrained by force; and this person, who had at first presented an evident obtusity of touch and an extraordinary contraction of the visual field, now exhibited an almost normal touch of three millimetres and a visual field enlarged to triple its extent when he was sober. (1900, n.p.)

The next day, not surprisingly, the young monarchist, once again had no recollection of events of the night before.

Lombroso's conclusion is that the "double personality" determined in other anarchists by misery or fanaticism was determined in this poor figure by alcohol. This is, for Lombroso, a real breakthrough. In his words:

> The fact helps us to explain how some inoffensive man may have a type of physiognomy quite similar to that of Ravachol, showing how often there are true criminals in potency, whose physiognomy, or rather the anomalies of it, bears a prophetic relation to the crime which breaks out on the first determining circumstance. And we have here another explanation of such contradictory characters as those of Ravachol, Caserio, and Luccheni, who, having been once well behaved, end by becoming criminals.

The reader might well ask, again, what the young confessor's criminality was based on since he committed no crime in this case (except perhaps false confession). Even more, though, there is no attempt at even the minimal analysis of social conditions or circumstances that might drive one to go from being well behaved to become a committed political activist.

Gli Anarchici

Lombroso takes up the focus on anarchism and crime in his commentary with the famous work Criminal Man (1911) produced with his daughter Lombroso-Ferrero. In Gli Anarchici ("The Anarchists") Lombroso suggests that if anarchist theories are not so absurd (a significant shift in perspective, according anarchist ideas some respect) the methods adopted by anarchists certainly are. This condemnation of methods is based on Lombroso's belief that all reforms should be introduced only very gradually.

These methods, absurd for Lombroso, explain why the crimes of anarchists are said to mingle with ordinary crimes (such as theft). It also explains why "with a few exceptions, anarchists are recruited from among ordinary criminals, lunatics, and insane criminals" (1911, 306). In Gli Anarchici,

Lombroso repeats the claimed proportions of occurrence of the criminal type among anarchists noted in the earlier work "The Physiognomy of the Anarchists" of 1891. Nowhere is there any acknowledgement that "ordinary criminals" might have good, well earned, reasons for developing an affinity for anti-authoritarian perspectives or for opposing institutions of authority. Neither is there any hint of recognition that lunatic and insane designations might be in any way flawed or arbitrary or misapplied.

In Gli Anarchici, Lombroso proposes:

> The majority of anarchists possess the passions and vices peculiar to ordinary criminals: impulsiveness, love of orgies, lack of natural affections and moral sense; and similar intellectual manifestations, such as slang, ballads, tattooing, hieroglyphics. But there are a greater number of genuine epileptic and hysterical subjects, lunatics, and indirect suicides among anarchists than among ordinary criminals; greater, too, is the proportion of criminals from passion. (1911, 306)

This notably includes a range of social choices, preferences, and expressions. Nothing is done to engage the anarchist critique of monogamy and support for sexual liberation expressed in acceptance of orgies. The accusations against slang and ballads can only properly be situated as part of a snobbish class arrogance that Lombroso regularly and openly displays.

Lombroso does note, though, that anarchists find violence distasteful. He even suggests, without following the implications of it that anarchists have disassociated themselves from those engaging in random acts of violence.

That there is purpose in anarchist crimes is reflected in the way anarchists stand up for and address their actions when captured, as in court statements. As Lombroso himself suggests:

> The crimes of these passionate criminals are always accomplished single-handed; they always surrender to the police immediately afterwards and make no attempt to defend themselves. On the contrary, when in court, they frequently give a lucid explanation of the motives that have induced them to commit their crimes and affront the penalty with stoicism. (1911, 307)

Lombroso maintains as sense that anarchists are of a different character than ordinary criminals. He states, with something of a complimentary tone: "In spite of the fact that anarchists are frequently criminals, their ideas, although often absurd, imply a greater elevation of character than the cynical apathy in which the worst types of criminals are sunk" (1911, 307). Lombroso also advocates for different responses to anarchist crime. Punishment is, to be sure, still in order. Violence, as in capital violence, must be meted out cautiously against the anarchists. Not due to any concerns for human rights or dignity expressed by Lombroso but rather to avoid the making of martyrs or the sparking of broad outrage. As Lombroso concludes Gli Anarchici:

> Instead of combating violence by violence and dealing out death sentences with a prodigality almost rivalling that of anarchists themselves, the authorities should segregate the most dangerous types or relegate them to distant islands, and adopt exile as a penalty for genuine criminals of passion. However, political liberty and some safety-valve, whereby lawless instincts may be turned into harmless channels, are the best methods for preventing anarchism. Constitutional government and freedom of speech and the press may go a long way towards combating anarchism; but the restoration of popular tribunates, like those to which Rome owed her balance and tranquillity, would be still more efficacious. If the governing bodies were to favour, instead of hindering, the formation of such institutions, which tend to spring up everywhere and to voice the grievances of the people, just causes would not be abandoned exclusively to the advocacy of extremists. (1911, 307)

That the anarchists were not "common criminals," for Lombroso, is suggested by their, to his view, heroic deaths, as he outlines in "The Physiognomy of the Anarchists." Never mind that these were state orchestrated murders for the most.

Conclusion

Clearly Lombroso was able to use his "analysis" of anarchists and Communards to gain access to resources of the Paris police. He was also able to present himself as an "expert" analyst, despite the clearly political nature of his work. Lombroso was able to use his profiling of anarchists to build cultural, or "scientific," capital for himself and to establish his position as a reliable scientist and policy advisor. He was, even more, of course, able to parlay his political posturing against anarchists into a prominent, viable, and highly rewarding career as a criminologist.

Lombroso professes a semi-theory of what he terms misonéique in social development. Society, according to Lombroso "has a horror of the new" (1897, 2). Thus anarchists are rendered, for Lombroso, as worse than criminal. They are an expression of that they which cannot be permitted. They are the horrible.

References

Lombroso, C. (1891). "Illustrative Studies in Criminal Anthropology. III. The Physiognomy of the Anarchists." *The Monist* 1(3): 336–343.

Lombroso, C. (1900). "A Paradoxical Anarchist." *Popular Science Monthly* 56, January. http://en.wikisource.org/wiki/Popular_Science_Monthly/Volume_56/January_1900/A_Paradoxical_Anarchist

Lombroso, C. (1911). *Criminal Man*. New York: G. P. Putnam's Sons.

Part II
Contemporary Voices on Alternatives to Punitive Justice Within Anarchist Criminology

4. "Freedom First": Pursuing Abolition Through Supporting Prisoner Resistance

COLLEEN HACKETT AND BEN TURK

> This monster—the monster they've engendered in me will return to torment its maker, from the grave, the pit, the profoundest pit… They won't defeat my revenge, never, never. I'm part of a righteous people who anger slowly, but rage undammed. We'll gather at his door in such a number that the rumbling of our feet will make the earth tremble…
>
> —George Jackson, *Soledad Brother* (1970)

Introduction

On February 1, 2017, prisoners at Vaughn Correctional Center near Smyrna, Delaware took guards hostage and occupied a portion of the facility. Their public statement demanded education, rehabilitation programming, and budget transparency. They also spoke of conditions worsening since the recent presidential election and they expected that trend to continue and escalate under the Trump regime (Thompson, 2017). The uprising at Vaughn follows years of growing prisoner resistance, which reached a national level on September 9th of 2016, the 45th anniversary of the Attica rebellion. These revolts, protests, and strikes signal a return to militant post-civil rights era opposition to prison and white supremacy at large. The monster George Jackson spoke of was created by the white supremacist politics of confinement and carceral torture and, after several decades, that monster continues to haunt every cellblock, special housing unit, and supermax. Prison rebellions have great power to draw out the inherent contradictions between the racist origins of carceral power and the "postracial" liberal democratic society that purports to offer equality and fairness.

As anarchists, we assert that the capitalist, patriarchal, and white supremacist state construct carceral "solutions" to social problems in order to maintain status quo interests and to subdue ungovernable populations (Davis, 2003; Gilmore, 2015; Simon, 2009). The U.S. chooses to rely on prisons not due to a lack of awareness, but because the prison system ensures the maintenance and reproduction of exploitative social arrangements. Dominant approaches to prison abolition praxis tend to focus on shifting this reliance on incarceration by developing and demonstrating the superiority of community-based alternatives to prison (CR10 Publications Collective, 2008; McLeod, 2015). Prison abolition scholars offer nuanced understandings and theories on the shape of state power and repression in the United States, particularly as it is informed by settler colonialist logics of confinement and disappearance (Dayan, 2013; Muhammad, 2011; Nichols, 2014). The anarchist and prison rebels' approach to abolition seeks to augment and accelerate these strategies through direct action. The praxis of leveraging this power is underdeveloped within the abolitionist cause, which would benefit greatly not only from increased awareness, but active support of and participation in prisoner-led resistance actions. We must not merely convince society to turn away from carcerality, but to remove the choice altogether; we must render carcerality impossible by amplifying prisoners' ungovernability and creating a perpetual "crisis of legitimacy" for prison officials (Habermas, 1975; Irwin and Simon, 2013).

This contribution will outline the importance of emboldening prisoners' resistance efforts against state-sponsored terror and patterns of degradation. Prisoners provide an informed and grounded analytic of state repression, carceral power, and resistance that is invaluable to abolitionist thought and strategy. We argue that prison uprisings, rebellions, and prisoners' analytics are integral to constructing a more robust abolitionist ethic and praxis. Through this framework, we analyze the ways in which prisoners' organizing efforts of the past decade have helped to propel the urgency of the abolitionist project, while signaling an opportunity for collaboration in making visible the inherent "cracks" of a system built on a long legacy of racialized violence. We first discuss the nefarious connections between prisons, slavery, and colonialism before transitioning into current efforts prisoners are making in resisting the white supremacist politics of confinement and pacification, specifically in how prison rebels are creating counterhegemonic civic spaces. We concretely discuss examples of prison rebellions and direct actions undertaken by prisoners in the last decade to illustrate our points.

The Afterlife of Slavery and Colonization

Slavery 400 years ago, slavery today. It's the same but with a new name.
—Ruchell Cinque Magee, *SF Bay View* (2008)

The enduring legacy of white supremacy has persisted despite the abolition of more overt forms of racial control. Saidiya Hartman refers to this continuous haunting as the "afterlife of slavery"; racial terror transforms and its contemporary manifestations are "skewed life chances, limited access to health and education, premature death, incarceration, and impoverishment" (2008, p. 6). The insidious cause of this afterlife is the deep entrenchment of a racial calculus that hierarchicalizes social value based on one's closeness to or distance from whiteness. The European colonizers' constructions of the Indigenous as "savage" and the African slave as a "non-person" created a durable outsider status that has since been legally transmuted and imposed upon populations deemed undesirable, or in some cases, less than human (Fanon, 2008; Wynter, 2003). The residual echoes of the "other" are felt from the initial colonial contact with Indigenous Americans and Africans, through to the slave holds, plantations, "Indian" removal policies and reservations, Jim Crow segregation policies, boarding schools, Japanese internment camps, conversion therapy, redlining, and the war on drugs. The ghosts of slavery and colonization continue to possess American logics and institutional life, animating a carceral grid of captivity and disappearance (Deer, 2015; Hernández, 2017). Yet, this system of conquest extends beyond the original targets of settler colonialism and chattel slavery; it applies a "foundational eliminatory logic" for anyone who is unable or unwilling to conform to a white supremacist heteropatriarchal society, but especially Indigenous and racialized communities, along with houseless, poor, and/or queer populations (Hernández, 2017; see also, Nichols, 2014, Rodríguez, 2008; Simpson, 2014).

The white supremacist project in the United States, one fueled by racist logics and institutions, along with punitive (white) sentiments, now uses the prison system as its primary tool in enforcing an eliminatory logic. The penal leviathan is a result of a turn in the politics of domination, one that relies on carceral-punitive apparatuses—incarceration in particular—to criminalize those opposing state repression and ongoing racial terror. During the Civil Rights Movement, conservatives linked civil disobedience to criminality and "lawlessness," rather than to a defined political movement (Alexander, 2012). With later liberatory struggles, like the Black Panther Party, the American Indian Movement, the Black Liberation Army, the Brown Berets and related Chicanx struggles, and the Weather Underground, the U.S. employed an aggressive assaultive against political dissidents through the FBI's notorious

COINTELPRO (Churchill and Vander Wall, 2001; Abu-Jamal and Fernández, 2014). The state's disruption of civil rights and liberation movements set the stage for a much larger campaign of mass incarceration through the ideological framework of "colorblindness" (Alexander, 2012; Berger, 2014; Taylor, 2016). Under this façade, elitist political discourses marked the targets of carceral confinement as "deserving" of its consequences rather than victims of institutionalized racial control. Criminalization represents a pinnacle of state repression, attempting to control unruliness and prevent disruptions to "law and order" while maintaining status quo racial and class interests.

The state's ability to use criminalization to control social movements and "unruly" populations became a historical possibility because of the firm embeddedness of racialized violence within the democratic order of the U.S. (Dayan, 2013; Gilmore, 2000). The juridical fixture of racial terror is perhaps the most apparent with the passage of the Thirteenth Amendment, in which the U.S. abolished slavery except as punishment for a crime. And, though the analytic connections between slavery and prison are popularly being embraced by a more mainstream audience as of late, Black liberationists and their accomplices have acutely understood and observed the entanglement of anti-blackness in our legal structures soon after slavery was supposedly abolished, and up until the present day. As famed sociologist W.E.B. Du Bois notes,

> Slavery was not abolished even after the Thirteenth Amendment. There were four million freedmen and most of them on the same plantation, doing the same work that they did before emancipation.... (2013 [1935], p. 166)

Du Bois and other slavery abolitionists understood that until the political order that legalized, condoned, and maintained chattel slavery was unmade, equity and liberation could not become a possibility. Yet in the aftermath of slavery, Black codes and the convict leasing program preserved racialized patterns of domination; the "nonperson" status of slaves—the legal dispossession of personhood—was transmuted to the "civil death" status of criminals (Dayan, 2013).

A description of the modern carceral state would be incomplete without an examination of its white supremacist origins and the enduring continuity of racialized violence. The technologies and logics of domination slightly change their form, but the core function remains: racialized social control and the preservation of a white supremacist order. The Thirteenth Amendment allows slavery to live on through criminal punishments, which were aggressively ramped up in the civil rights and Black/Chicanx/Indigenous power era, leaving the United States with the sordid reputation of being the global leader in incarceration rates. The prison system has its power in imposing the antebellum era notion of "social death" upon its captives. The "legal engines of dispossession," enabled by white supremacy and mechanized by the criminal legal system, inflict this social death upon those deemed to be criminal, which is the "loss of status so extreme that life ceases to be politically relevant" (Dayan, 2013, p. 60). The official narratives that frame "criminals" as having poor moral character, being highly dangerous, and needing redemption and/or transformation legitimate the removal of criminalized peoples from the body politic in order to prevent "contamination." This social death process marks a denial of civil and political personhood for the prisoner—which, when viewed in the aggregate, results in the dispossession of racialized communities to their self-determining authority and sovereign claims to governance. Yet, this legal disenfranchisement is not totalizing and, as described throughout the rest of this chapter, currently incarcerated prisoners are resisting this social death and creatively crafting new, collective forms of political personhood.

Prison Revolts: Resisting Civil Death, Creating Political Spaces

> I urge each and every one of you to imagine yourself drowning… All your training goes out the window, but your survival instincts emerge. You were taught to not flail about when drowning, yet at the moment of drowning, you do flail. Was I not to flail? Was I supposed to accept death by suffocation in [this] sweat box?
>
> - -Greg Curry, *Repression Breeds Resistance* (2014)

On September 9, 2016, the 45th anniversary of the Attica uprising, prison rebels engaged in diverse protests against their captivity, exploitation, and the systems of capitalism and white supremacy. According to estimates gathered by prisoner supporters, there were over 57,000 prisoners affected by the action that impacted at least 46 facilities across the nation.[1] Solidarity Research calculated that the strike cost the California prison system alone $636,068 in revenue each day (2016). The events of September 9th also broke through the typical media blockade around prisoner resistance, gaining coverage in mainstream national and local papers, as well as many alternative news sources (SPR, 2016a). This was by far the largest prisoner protest in U.S. history, and the first to be nationally coordinated. Prisoners' actions were supported by robust outside protests. Solidarity actions around the 9th and days following included marches, blockades, noise demos, general assemblies, letter writing, phone calls to officials, and an attack on a local Democratic Party office in Bloomington, Indiana (It's Going Down, 2016). The National Lawyer's Guild, The Industrial Workers of the World, Critical Resistance, and various other organizations endorsed and supported the strike and attempted to coordinate legal defense and public awareness campaigns for prisoners facing retaliation (SPR, 2016b).

The September 9th strike came after years of expanded mass organizing within U.S. prisons. In 2010, prisoners in Georgia staged a state-wide work strike (Dixon, 2010) which was the largest in history, until 2016. In 2011 and 2013 California prisoners engaged in massive rolling hunger strikes involving 30,000 participants (St. John, 2013). These protests inspired lasting prisoner unity in the CA prison system plagued with gang violence and racial divisions (Jamaa, 2017). In Alabama, prisoners initiated a steady stream of hunger strikes, work stoppages, and rebellions beginning in 2014 and continuing to the present. They also formed an organization entitled The Free Alabama Movement and outlined a strategy against prison slavery they called "Let the Crops Rot in the Fields" (FAM, 2015). The Industrial Workers of the World, at the urging of Black anarchist and former prisoner Lorenzo KomBoa Ervin, formed an Incarcerated Worker's Organizing Committee (IWOC), which quickly burgeoned into a national organization taking a key role in the September 9th prisoner strike.

Prisoner resistance is complex and myriad. Though in this chapter we focus on mass prisoner movements that are collectivized and either statewide or national, we want to acknowledge that we are not capturing the entirety of prisoner resistance. Much of the academic and activist literature, as well as media accounts, focus on uprisings that take the form of hunger strikes, work stoppages, or violent rebellions. We want to make it abundantly clear that we do not believe this is the only type of prisoner resistance or set of oppositional tactics. Diffused and informal acts of defiance are everyday occurrences. We assert that simply surviving in the brutal prison context is a political act, which becomes a useful framework when considering the resilience of prisoners with neurodivergence, those with different physical abilities, and those experiencing gendered oppression, such as women and trans prisoners. Yet, there are also many instances of incarcerated subpopulations resisting the prison system through political channels that are underemphasized: forming study groups, making resistance art, and raising public awareness about women's, trans, and LGBQAI issues in prison (Law, 2012; Black and Pink, 2017). Though the scope of this paper cannot allow a more in-depth inquiry into these different political efforts, we welcome more support efforts and scholarly inquiry into the wide array of prisoner resistance with a particular focus on gender, sexuality, and ableist oppression.

Carceral-punitive apparatuses seek to inscribe an "otherness" onto the bodies of those captured within its cages, prompting prisoners to employ a "strategy of visibility" (Berger, 2014), whereby they utilize the power of the pen—and at times, the sword—to reassert their human dignity and substantive need for human relations within and beyond the prison walls. In affirming their subjectivities through rhetorically connecting with collective movements, such as #BlackLivesMatter and trans liberation projects, prisoners demand the recognition of their political subjectivities (Hasan and Keith, 2015). The recent string of uprisings demonstrate the ways that prisoners continue to collectively resist the ontological and social death that comes from the terror of state control over prisoners' bodies, labor, and identity (Cacho, 2012; Rodríguez, 2008).

Much like the civil rights and Black power era of prison organizing, contemporary prison rebels use a framework and analytic of slavery in their critique of the prison regime and their conditions of confinement (Berger, 2014). This rhetoric of enslavement was particularly salient in the historic September 9th, 2016 prison strikes that demanded prisoners to stop working on prison plantations and to—literally and metaphorically—"let the crops rot in the field" (FAM, 2015). We will discuss how prisoners' frameworks first focused on forced labor and abysmal working conditions before we move to prisoners' understandings of prison slavery as also being about the state's attempts at controlling and warehousing bodies and also about the state's attempt to strip prisoners of their political voice.

Slavery as Forced Labor: Work Stoppages and Strikes

Many of the prisoner demands from the last decade focus on improved working conditions and wages (FOM, 2016; Dixon, 2010; IWOC, 2016). Pay for prison labor ranges from an average of $0.93 per day to none at all (Blau and Grinberg, 2016). This is often central to media coverage of the strike, and can lead to an assumption that prisoners are organizing for better jobs and better pay within their captivity, but it is important to recognize this rhetoric in terms of strategy as much as goals. The Free Alabama Movement has been explicit about this from the start, stating "The numbers support our contention that "MONEY" is the motive...[t]herefore, an economical response is our most effective strategy" in an article that lists five broad demands, four of which are aimed at reducing sentences and releasing prisoners (Amun, 2015). Refusing labor is often a tactic employed to gain freedom and basic human rights. This is a Call to End Slavery in America, the title of the call to action for September 9th, illustrates the broader goals of a work stoppage:

Our protest against prison slavery is a protest against the school to prison pipeline, a protest against police terror, a protest against post-release controls.

When we abolish slavery, they'll lose much of their incentive to lock up our children, they'll stop building traps to pull back those who they've released. When we remove the economic motive and grease of our forced labor from the US prison system, the entire structure of courts and police, of control and slave-catching must shift to accommodate us as humans, rather than slaves (SPR, 2016d).

This analysis understands that by withholding labor power, prisoners assert themselves as full subjects and demand a place in the political economy of a nation built on its ability to deny them such.

A prisoner work stoppage does not merely impact the prison factories, denying profits to either private companies or state industries that operate within the prison, it also shuts down the facility itself. Relatively few prisoners work in the factories, instead fulfilling most of the jobs needed to clean, maintain, and operate correctional facilities, along with feeding and caring for other prisoners—particularly those who are aging or unable to care for themselves. During a work stoppage, correctional officers must take over prisoners' jobs. They do so resentfully, and at great cost to the prison. The correctional officers will do the work exceptionally poorly, both as retaliation and because of the sudden expansion of job responsibilities. This adds images of unsanitary conditions, inadequate meals, and cruel negligence to the public narrative of the strike (Speri, 2016a). Prison administrators also resort to paying officers overtime or bringing in work release prisoners to replace the strikers (Turk, 2016a). The costs of these responses, in terms of finances, public legitimacy, and ability to maintain order are unsustainable in any correctional institution. Anarchist prisoner Sean Swain argues that a well-supported prisoner work stoppage lasting more than 30 days would likely bankrupt most state budgets (2007). This is the economic impact prisoners hope to leverage by refusing slavery and withholding their labor power (Turk, 2016b).

Slavery as Physiological Evisceration: Fighting with the Body

The analytic currency of slavery offers more than just a critique of coerced work and conditions of work. Prisoners also contest the ways in which their enslavement involves state control over their bodies. In commemorating the September 9th strikes, the editors of True Leap Press remark on the function of physiological evisceration through imprisonment:

> While the economic dimensions of the prison industrial complex are indeed important to recognize and challenge; its primary function is to warehouse and disappear poor and working class Black (and in many regions Brown and Indigenous) people. Its purpose is to immobilize and liquidate white America's "undesirables" from society—to render Black and Brown people civilly and socially dead. (2016)

One egregious example of corporeal exploitation include the practice of non-consensual tubal ligation procedures done by the California Department of Corrections between 1997 and 2010, which effectively sterilized up to 250 women prisoners, most of them Black and Latina (California Coalition for Women Prisoners, 2013). This state control of reproductive systems strongly resembles eugenics programs that centered women as the bearers of societal "contamination." It additionally hearkens back to the institution of slavery in that it encompasses more than just slaveholders demanding forced labor; rather, the slave's body becomes subject to inhumane medical procedures and the slaveholders' own personal objectifications.

This project of liquidating undesirable bodies extends into the belly of certain prisons. Secure housing units (SHU), administrative control (AC), supermax prisons, and other forms of segregated housing create more tightly confined spaces that are essentially "prisons within prisons" (Gómez, 2006). Prisoners confined in long term solitary confinement experience a "living death," with expanded restrictions on movement, access to space, communication, visitation, food and other commissary items, reading materials, legal resources, income opportunities, education and religious programming, and medical assistance. In segregation, a prison rebel's protest options, like everything else, are severely restricted, leading prisoners to engage in desperate acts that put their own lives and well being at risk (Swain, 2015; Mai-Duc, 2015). Segregation often involves steady harassment, surveillance, threats, and psychological torture until the prisoner is broken down to involuntary neuro-biological responses. Prison authority aspires to have absolute control of captive bodies in a project of disappearance, liquidation, and rendering the target socially dead. Every year, approximately 185 state and federal prisoners commit suicide and an unknown number attempt suicide (Noonan et al., 2013). Given the invasive and destructive aspects of prison authority, we must admit these desperate and tragic acts, including suicide, are also a form of resistance that ought to inspire an urgent devotion to not merely phasing prison out, but ending it categorically and immediately, regardless of social costs. At times, prisoners only have their bodies to fight back with.

An example in a Wisconsin prison illuminates the practice of corporeal resistance. In June of 2016, more than thirty prisoners in the AC unit in Waupun Wisconsin declared a hunger strike. Afraid to use the phrase "hunger strike" because of Wisconsin Department of Corrections' (WI DOC) reputation for harsh reprisals, they called it a "food refusal protest" which they named Dying to Live (FFUP, 2016). WI DOC quickly lived up to their reputation. After only ten days of refusing food, prison officials had deterred most of the hunger strikers. To break the few remaining, they sought and received judicial approval to force feed the prisoners (Hall, 2016). The hunger strikers persisted, enduring dozens of painful and high-risk violations of their bodily autonomy. Prison staff shoved tubes down restrained prisoners' noses and poured liquid nutrition into their stomachs against their will. When the method failed on Joshua Scolman because of a deviated septum, the DOC doctor threatened to surgically install a feeding tube directly to his stomach (Swan, 2016). He quit the protest instead. Once prison staff determined that administering three force feedings a day would be too laborious, they began a regimen of refeeding, where the prisoner would be allowed to starve and severely dehydrate for a few days and then be force-fed a large quantity in one sitting, which shocks the system (Turk, 2016c). Force feeding is not medically necessary after only 10 days, and the refeeding regimen WI DOC subjected prisoners to risks heart failure and increases dehydration and serious injury (Inglis-Arkell, 2015). This specific case demonstrates that the prison regime is ideologically opposed to allowing prison rebels to exercise authority over their own lives and will stop at nothing to assert its exclusive dominion in controlling prisoners' bodies.

Slavery as Voicelessness: Asserting Political Personhood

The third way in which prisoners frame their captivity as slavery is demonstrating how the prison regime attempts to deny them their voice through the use of various social pacification tools, brute force, censorship, and managerial democracy. By infantalizing criminals as not knowing what is "good" for them or demonizing criminals as evil or dangerous, the prison regime attempts to undermine the legitimacy of prisoners' political personhood. Many prisoners assert their capacities for political agency, often through writing treatises and political analyses, forming study groups, and issuing demands. Kinetik Justice, Dhati Khalid, and Melvin Ray, for example, formed an impromptu study group in Alabama prisons, hearkening back to the civil rights era emergence of prisoner-led ethnic studies groups. This was the genesis of the Free Alabama Movement (*The Thread*, 2016).

Prisons are sites where any form of protest or organizing is considered illegitimate. Prison authorities have broad freedoms to monitor and censor communication via the mail, phone, and visitation. They can move prisoners into isolation and cancel education and religious programming with the creation of a potentially fabricated disciplinary report. Despite these restrictions, prisoners continue to organize and brazenly risk punishment to assert their political personhood and pursue their organizing efforts. Siddique Abdullah Hasan, a survivor of the Lucasville Uprising, who has been incarcerated for most of his life and has spent the last 23 years in solitary confinement battling his death sentence is, despite these deprivations, a skilled political organizer. Hasan was the first prisoner to risk publicly speaking about his role in planning the September 9th national work stoppage and protest (Hasan, 2016), He, like the Free Alabama Prisoners mentioned above, has suffered greatly to maintain and expand his organizing access and capacity. Starting with a 13-day hunger strike in 2010, undertaken with two other death sentenced Lucasville Uprising survivors, in which he won access to partial contact visits (after 19 years without touching another human who wasn't putting handcuffs on him), access to the law library, increased recreation and phone time, Hasan and his comrades have steadily expanded their ability to contact the outside world (Democracy Now!, 2011). By pushing the boundaries and being as persistent as the prison machine designed to wear people down, Hasan has successfully had his voice featured in numerous national media outlets, including the popular National Public Radio show "On Point" and an episode of the Netflix documentary "Captives" (Ashbrook, 2016, Blake, 2016). In response to these efforts and other forays into public political venues, Hasan has been sanctioned repeatedly, responding with hunger strikes (Speri, 2016b; Sonenstein, 2017). From mid-August 2016, until the end of May 2017, Hasan will have had phone access restricted for 210 out of 280 days based on conduct reports that were either fabricated or improperly filed. During that time he responded with two hunger strikes, refusing food for a total of 45 days.

This assertion of political personhood can take the form of confrontational insurgency, one that strikes back "against the respectable, non-scandalous, legitimated forms" of protests (Rodríguez, 2016). At Holman Correctional in Alabama, prisoners made gains through a diverse array of tactics, between March and November of 2016. Between the Free Alabama Movement's nonviolent approach of work stoppages, less organized uprisings, occupations, and arsons, as well as frequent attacks on staff including the stabbing of multiple guards and one warden, Holman was on the leading edge of crisis in the prison system (Blinder, 2016; Denton, 2016). At the end of September, an entire shift of correctional officers refused to come to work, leaving the prison administration to perform daily operations themselves. Kinetik Justice described the situation for Democracy Now!:

> Right now the commissioner is passing out trays. Warden Peterson is pulling the cart. Deputy Commissioner Cullum: passing out trays. Every cell, he passing out the tray. I can't believe this. To they black slide-in shoes, brown knitted pants, white tweed shirt with the collar bust open, sweatin at the temples. Is real. No officer came to work, they completely bumped on the administration. No more will they be pawns in the game. In our time, it's going down. (2016)

The image of wardens and superintendents walking the halls and passing out trays best demonstrates the power of sustained, diverse and well-supported prisoner resistance to render prison facilities untenable. More support and participation in these organizing efforts can extend the length and depth of the prison's crises. FAM's explicit non-violent approach has been rejected by other Alabama prisoners, both in word and deed (Kimble, 2017), but unlike many "free-world" pacifists, FAM has never denounced or sided with the authorities against rebels who take violent action; indeed, they have consistently helped raise awareness of uprisings and occupations. This shows a more mature and sophisticated approach to organizing than many protest movements on the outside.

By asserting themselves as political actors, accessing media coverage, and creating crises within the prisons, rebels drag prison officials into a competition for credibility. Events in Michigan around September 9th demonstrate what strong and well-supported prisoner resistance can cost a prison system in terms of legitimacy. During the spring and summer of 2016, Michigan prisoners engaged in a series of meal boycotts to demonstrate unity against conditions in multiple facilities (SPR, 2016e; Egan, 2016a). Then, on September 9th, prisoners at Kinross CI in Kincheloe, MI refused to work and the next day, organized a nonviolent march around the yard. They refused to re-enter the buildings until the administration met demands regarding specific changes to conditions in the prison. At the same time, outside protests took an intersection in downtown Lansing in solidarity with the strike (Ross, 2016). Chris Gautz, a public information officer from the Michigan DOC is one of the few prison officials who talked to the media when the strikes were going on. He was on a panel for Al Jazeera English's "The Stream" program with Kinetik Justice and Phillip Ruiz of IWOC. Gautz claimed that Michigan doesn't have trouble with prisoner protests, and when asked what happens when prisoners refuse to work, he said "Michigan prisoners are not forced to work." Kinetik and Ruiz pushed back expressing doubt about Gautz's statements (Stream, 2016). Shortly thereafter, word of the protest in Kinross became public, and The Detroit Free Press shared prisoner's stories of the state's response to their work refusal. After being promised by the warden that their demands would be met, the prisoners returned to the cellblock, where they were attacked. An Emergency Response Team entered the block and fired tear gas guns at prisoners at point blank range, dragged prisoners back to the yard, hog tied them for hours in the rain, and transferred them to other facilities across the state (MAPS, 2017; Egan, 2016b).

Outside supporters with Michigan Abolition Prisoner Solidarity (MAPS) and IWOC coordinated interviews between family members and journalists, and continue to support prisoners with call-in campaigns and news releases about hunger strikes and resistance from prisoners in segregation (It's Going Down, 2017). The crisis created by prisoners and augmented by outside support efforts dragged officials into the public light where they tried and failed to legitimize the prison. The work of MAPS in this effort is at once essentially important, strategically effective, and easily generalizable. It does not require special talents or extraordinary risks, merely a willingness to engage authentically with the trauma of dire circumstances prisoners find themselves in, some straightforward writing, and attention to basic administrative, outreach and communication tasks, all skills which are relatively easy to learn by doing.

Conclusion: Making Prisons Impossible

> To treat us this way is wrong, evil and unsustainable socially. Stand with us. Lend your voices, your labor, and your ideas to this historical work. We can win, but only with you all by our sides. In the final analysis, this is a struggle to determine the nature of humanity itself… Until we win or don't lose.
>
> —Dorrough, Denham, and Robinson, *SF Bay View*, 2012

The prison rebellions of the past decade, and especially the nationwide strike on September 9th, exploit this dependency to illuminate the lived crises of prisons. They throw into question the legitimacy of the state and call forth the contradictions of "democracy." Positing a multidimensional framework of slavery to understand the politics of their confinement, prisoners awaken the public to the inherent problems with caging life and its deep roots in white supremacy. With the increasingly popular historicization of the prison as a site of deeply embedded racial terror, there are new revolutionary possibilities—if done in conjunction with prisoners held captive.

Supporting and generalizing prisoner resistance requires more resources than current solidarity organizations are capable of or have access to. Though we applaud the many abolitionist projects around the world and the constructive possibilities they hold in crafting a new social imaginary, we urge organizers and scholars to act with prisoners in actively abolishing the prison system. Eroding the logic, credibility, and power of prisons is a matter of defiant survival and asserting personhood on a daily and hourly basis for prisoners. We want readers to ask the question, how can our support efforts better match prisoners' commitments to crumbling the prison system?

We assert that supporting large-scale actions described in this chapter is just the start. Prisoners called for another national action on August 19, 2017, with a greater focus on mass outside support (IamWe, 2016), but steady, reliable, and long-term support projects are also essential. Developing relationships with prisoners establishes an infrastructure and network of resistance across prison fences. There are many programs already in place that could use human capital, as well as financial support. Such efforts include books or zines to prisoners, penpal programs, prisoner publications, classes inside prisons focusing on political education or radical trauma work, and workshops or discussion meetups in the community[2]. These support efforts help prisoners organize themselves, spread their knowledge of the horrors of the carceral regime, assert their political agency, bring attention to their particular cases, and importantly, connect with "free-world" abolitionist projects and scholarship. Actively organizing with our captive comrades to refuse the carceral regime is an essential part of crafting a society that rejects white supremacy and colonialism.

Notes

1. Lack of transparency in most state prison systems makes accurate numbers very difficult to acquire. Organizers from *supportprisonerresistance.net* used the following method:

   > We have tracked 46 prisons and jails that experienced some kind of disruption between September 8th and 21st. This total includes both lockdowns reported by officials … and reports of protests from prisoners and supporters (some of which did not lead to lockdowns or full strikes). Of these, 31 facilities experienced a lock-down, suspension or full strike for at least 24 hours. Those 31 facilities house approximately 57,000 people. (SPR, 2016c)

2. Some examples include: Books and zines to Prisoners (Chicago Books to Women in Prison, Prison Books in Chapel Hill NC, Books Through Bars in New York, Midwest Pages to Prisoners in Bloomington IN); Penpal programs (Anarchist Black Cross, Black and Pink); Prisoner publications (The *San Francisco Bayview*, *Fire Inside*, *Unstoppable!*, *The Incarcerated Worker*, *Black and Pink*, *The Abolitionist*, *Wildfire*); Classes inside prisons (WEBS of Support).

References

Abu-Jamal, M., & J. Fernández. (2014). "Locking up black dissidents and punishing the poor: The roots of mass incarceration in the U.S." *Socialism and Democracy,* 28(3), 1–14.

Alexander, M. (2012). *The new Jim Crow: Mass incarceration in the age of color blindness.* New York, NY: The New Press.

Amun, Kinetic Justice. (2015). "A flicker turns into a flame: Alabama's prisoners want change." *The Incarcerated Worker,* 1(1). Retrieved from https://iwoc.noblogs.org/files/2015/08/2015-1-Incarcerated-Worker-February-2015-read.pdf

Ashbrook, T. (2016). "American prison inmates, on strike." *On Point.* September 28, 2016. Retrieved from http://www.wbur.org/onpoint/2016/09/28/prison-strike-prison-reform

Berger, Dan. (2014). *Captive nation: Black prison organizing in the civil rights era.* Chapel Hill, NC: The University of North Carolina Press.

Black and Pink. (2017). "Purpose and Analysis. Black and Pink: Prison Abolition Now!" Retrieved from http://www.blackandpink.org/purpose-analysis/

Blake, Meredith. (2016). The Netflix documentary series 'Captive' takes a gripping look at hostage crises across the globe. *Los Angeles Times.* December 8, 2016. Retrieved from http://www.latimes.com/entertainment/tv/la-et-st-captive-review-20161207-story.html

Blau, M., & Grinberg, E. (2016). Why US inmates launched a nationwide strike. *CNN.* October 31, 2016. Retrieved from http://www.cnn.com/2016/10/30/us/us-prisoner-strike/

Blinder, Alan. (2016). "Alabama prison uprisings come as state grapples with how to fix system." *New York Times.* March 15, 2016. Retrieved from https://www.nytimes.com/2016/03/16/us/alabama-prison-uprisings-come-as-state-grapples-with-how-to-fix-system.html?_r=0

Cacho, L. M. (2012). *Social death: Racialized rightlessness and the criminalization of the unprotected.* New York, NY: New York University Press.

California Coalition for Women Prisoners. (2013). "Stop CDCR Sterilizations!" *The Fire Inside.* 49, p. 7.

Churchill, W., & J. Vander Wall. (2001). *The COINTELPRO papers: Documents from the FBI's secret wars against dissent in the United States.* Cambridge, MA: South End Press.

CR10 Publications Collective. (2008). *Abolition now! Ten years of strategy and struggle against the prison industrial complex.* Oakland, CA: AK Press.

Curry, G. (2014). "Repression breeds resistance: Greg Curry on the Lucasville uprising and aftermath." *Zine.* Youngstown, OH: Author.

Davis, A. (2003). *Are Prisons Obsolete?* New York, NY: Seven Stories Press.

Dayan, C. (2013). *The law is a white dog: How legal rituals make and unmake persons.* Princeton, NJ: Princeton University Press.

Deer, S. (2015). *The beginning and end of rape: Confronting sexual violence in Native America.* Minneapolis, MN: University of Minnesota Press.

Democracy Now! (2011). "Prisoners at supermax Ohio penitentiary begin hunger strike to protest 17+ Year Solitary Confinement." *DemocracyNow.org.* January 4, 2011. Retrieved from https://www.democracynow.org/2011/1/4/prisoners_at_supermax_ohio_penitentiary_begin_hunger_strike_to_protest_17_year_solitary_confinement

Democracy Now! (2016). "Alabama guards stage work strike months after prisoner uprising at overcrowded holman facility." *DemocracyNow.org.* September 28, 2016. Retrieved from https://www.democracynow.org/2016/9/28/alabama_guards_stage_work_strike_months

Denton, J. (2016). "Prison labor strike in Alabama: We will no longer contribute to our own oppression." *SolitaryWatch.com.* May 5, 2016. Retrieved from http://solitarywatch.com/2016/05/05/prison-labor-strike-in-alabama-we-will-no-longer-contribute-to-our-own-oppression/

Dixon, B. (2010). "GA prison inmates stage 1-day peaceful strike today." *Black Agenda Report.* December 9, 2010. Retrieved from https://blackagendareport.com/content/ga-Prison-inmates-stage-1-day-peaceful-strike-today

Dorrough, Z., D. J. Heshima, & R. Kambui. (2012). "Feeling death at our heels: An update from the frontlines of struggle." *SF Bay View.* Retrieved from http://sfbayview.com/2012/01/feeling-death-at-our-heels-an-update-from-the-frontlines-of-the-struggle/

Du Bois, W. E. B. (2013). *Black reconstruction in America: Toward a history of the part which black folk played in the attempt to reconstruct democracy in America, 1860–1880.* New Brunswick, NJ: Transaction Publishers.

Egan, P. (2016a). *Prisoners protest food under new contractor Trinity.* Detroit Free Press. March 22, 2016. Retrieved from http://www.freep.com/story/news/local/michigan/2016/03/22/prisoners-protest-food-under-new-contractor-trinity/82120158/

Egan, P. (2016b). "Kinross inmate: Raid with pepper spray sparked vandalism." *Detroit Free Press.* October 4, 2016. Retrieved from http://www.freep.com/story/news/local/michigan/2016/10/04/kinross-inmate-raid-pepper-spray-sparked-vandalism/91469310/

FAM. (2015). "Let the crops rot in the fields." *Free Alabama Movement.* February 26, 2015. Retrieved from https://freealabamamovement.wordpress.com/2015/02/26/let-the-crops-rot-in-the-fields/

Fanon, F. (2008). *Black skin, white masks.* New York, NY: Grove Press.

FFUP. (2016). "Demands of food refusers June 2016, supported by petition sign." *Dying to Live.* June 1, 2016. Retrieved from https://solitarytorture.blogspot.com/2016/06/demands-of-food-refusers-june-2016.html

FOM. (2016). "Demands." *Free Ohio Movement.* October, 2016. Retrieved from freeohiomovement.org/files/Demands.pdf

Gilmore, K. (2000). "Slavery and prison: Understanding the connections." *Social Justice,* 27(3), 195–205.

Gilmore, R. W. (2015). "The worrying state of the anti-prison movement." *Social Justice,* Feb 2. Retrieved from http://www.socialjusticejournal.org/the-worrying-state-of-the-anti-prison-movement/

Gómez, A. E. (2006). "Resisting living death at Marion Federal Penitentiary, 1972." *Radical History Review,* 96, 58–86.

Habermas, J. (1975). *Legitimation crisis.* Boston, MA: Beacon Press.

Hall, D. (2016). "Wisconsin prison officials begin force feedings as solitary confinement protest continues." *WisconsinWatch.org* June 23, 2016. Retrieved from http://wisconsinwatch.org/2016/06/wisconsin-prison-officials-begin-force-feedings-as-solitary-confinement-protest-continues/

Hartman, S. (2008). *Lose your mother: A journey along the Atlantic slave route.* New York, NY: Farrar, Straus, and Giroux.

Hasan, S. A. (2016). "IWOC interview with Siddique Abdullah Hasan." April 17, 2016. Recording retrieved from https://youtu.be/OO5RODJXK1s

Hasan, S. A., & L. Keith. (2015). "Never dormant on death row." *[Zine.]* Youngstown, OH: Author.

Hernández, K. L. (2017). *City of inmates: Conquest, rebellion, and the rise of human caging in Los Angeles,* 1771–1965. Chapel Hill, NC: The University of North Carolina Press.

IamWe. (2016). Millions for prisoners human rights march. Retrieved from https://www.ushrnetwork.org/events/millions-prisoners-human-rights-march

Inglis-Arkell, Esther. (2015). *Here's what really happens when you force-feed someone.* Io9. April 21, 2015. Retrieved from http://io9.gizmodo.com/heres-what-really-happens-when-you-force-feed-someone-1699078018

Irwin, J., & J. Simon (2013). *The jail: Managing the underclass in American society.* Berkeley, CA: University of California Press.

It's Going Down. (2016). "Spreading the strike: Solidarity actions across North America for September 9th." *ItsGoingDown.org.* August 16, 2016. Retrieved from https://itsgoingdown.org/spreading-strike-solidarity-actions-across-north-america-september-9th

It's Going Down. (2017). "Harold Gonzales, Kinross Prisoner, to be released from solitary." *ItsGoingDown.org.* April 30, 2017. Retrieved from https://itsgoingdown.org/harold-gonzales-kinross-prisoner-released-solitary/

IWOC. (2016). "IWW's in Texas prisons planning work stoppages for early April." *IWW Incarcerated Worker's Organizing Committee.* April 4, 2016. Retrieved from https://iwoc.noblogs.org/post/2016/03/22/work-stoppages-in-texas-planned-for-early-april/

Jackson, G. (1994). *Soledad brother: The prison letters of George Jackson.* Chicago, IL: Lawrence Hill Books.

Jamaa, S. T. (2017). *PHRM: Our fifth year to the agreement to end hostilities: Recognize our humanity! Prisoner hunger strike solidarity.* April 18, 2017. Retrieved from https://prisonerhungerstrikesolidarity.wordpress.com/2017/04/18/phrm-our-fifth-year-to-the-agreement-to-end-hostilities-recognize-our-humanity/#more-11611

Kimble, M. (2017). "A look at the free Alabama movement." *Anarchy Live*! January 25, 2017. Retrieved from https://anarchylive.noblogs.org/post/2017/01/25/a-look-at-the-free-alabama-movement/

Law, V. (2012). *Resistance behind bars: The struggles of incarcerated women*, 2nd ed. Oakland, CA: PM Press.

Magee, R. C. (2017). "Ruchell Cinque Magee, sole survivor of the Aug 7, 1970, Courthouse Slave Rebellion." *SF Bay View.* Retrieved from: http://sfbayview.com/2017/02/ruchell-cinque-magee-sole-survivor-of-the-aug-7-1970-courthouse-slave-rebellion/

Mai-Duc, C. (2015). "Prison hunger strikes in the U.S. are few, and rarely successful." *Los Angeles Times.* August 5, 2015. Retrieved from http://www.latimes.com/la-na-nn-utah-prisoner-hunger-strike-20150804-story.html

MAPS. (2017). "What happened at Kinross?" *MichiganAbolition.org.* Retrieved from https://michiganabolition.org/timeline/

McLeod, A. (2015). "Prison abolition and grounded justice." *UCLA Law Review,* 62, 1156–1239.

Muhammad, K. G. (2011). *The condemnation of blackness: Race, crime, and the making of modern urban America*. Cambridge, MA: Harvard University Press.

Nichols, R. (2014). "The colonialism of incarceration." *Radical Philosophy Review*, 17(2), 435–455.

Noonan, M., H. Rohloff, & S. Ginder. (2013). "Mortality in local jails & state prisons, 2000–2013 – statistical tables." *Bureau of Justice Statistics*, 1–40.

Rodríguez, D. (2008). "'I would wish death on you…': Race, gender, and immigration in the globality of the U.S. prison regime." *Borders on Belonging: Gender and Immigration*, 6(3), 1–9.

Rodríguez, D. (2016). "Policing and the violence of white being: An interview with Dylan Rodríguez." *True Leap Press*. Retrieved from: https://trueleappress.wordpress.com/2016/08/30/policing-and-the-violence-of-white-being-an-interview-with-dylan-rodriguez/

Ross, M. (2016). "Prisoners' rights demonstrators block downtown traffic as part of nationwide protests." *The State News*. http://statenews.com. September 9, 2016. Retrieved from http://statenews.com/article/2016/09/prisoners-rights-demonstrators-block-downtown-Traffic-as-part-of-nationwide-protests

Simon, J. (2009). *Governing through crime: How the war on crime transformed American democracy and created a culture of fear.* New York, NY: Oxford University Press.

Simpson, A. (2014). *Mohawk interruptus: Political life across the borders of settler states.* Durham, NC: Duke University Press.

Solidarity Research. (2016). "Prison strike's financial impact in California." *Solidarity Research*. October 7, 2016. Retrieved from http://solidarityresearch.org/wp-content/uploads/2016/10/Prison-Strike-in-California-10-07-16.pdf

Sonenstein, B. (2017). "Ohio prisoner on hunger strike against punishment for Netflix documentary enters infirmary." *Shadowproof*. March 29, 2017. Retrieved from https://shadowproof.com/2017/03/29/hasan-enters-infirmary-netflix-documentary-captive/

Speri, A. (2016a). "Striking prisoners in Alabama accuse officials of using food as weapon." *The Intercept*. May 10, 2016. Retrieved from https://theintercept.com/2016/05/10/striking-prisoners-in-alabama-accuse-officials-of-using-food-as-weapon/

Speri, A. (2016b). "A prison strike organizer suffers retaliation for speaking with journalists." *The Intercept*. October 6, 2016. Retrieved from https://theintercept.com/2016/10/06/a-prison-strike-organizer-suffers-retaliation-for-speaking-with-journalists/

SPR. (2016a). *Coverage*. SupportPrisonerResistance.net. Retrieved from https://supportprisonerresistance.noblogs.org/coverage/

SPR. (2016b). *List of endorsements*. SupportPrisonerResistance.net. Retrieved from https://supportprisonerresistance.noblogs.org/endorsements/

SPR. (2016c). *Strike tracking and retaliation support*. SupportPrisonerResistance.net. September 1, 2016. Retrieved from https://supportprisonerresistance.noblogs.org/post/2016/09/01/strike-tracking-and-retaliation-support/

SPR. (2016d). *Call to action*. SupportPrisonerResistance.net. April 1, 2016. Retrieved from https://supportprisonerresistance.noblogs.org/post/2016/04/01/announcement-of-nationally-coordinated-prisoner-workstoppage-for-sept-9-2016/

SPR. (2016e). *"This was about unity": A wave of protest spreads through the Michigan prison system*. SupportPrisonerResistance.net. April 20, 2016. Retrieved from https://supportprisonerresistance.noblogs.org/post/2016/04/20/286

St. John, P. (2013). "California prison officials say 30,000 inmates refuse meals." *LA Times*. http://articles.latimes.com/2013/jul/08/local/la-me-pc-ff-california-prison-officials-acknowledge-hunger-strike-20130708

Stream, T. (2016). "The labour rights fight in US prisons." *The Stream*. September 26, 2016. Retrieved from https://www.youtube.com/watch?v=3RjCqn_F9ck

Swain, S. (2007). "Each one, teach one interview series: Sean Swain / Anthony Rayson." *[zine]*. Chicago, IL: South Chicago Zine Distro.

Swain, S. (2015). "Direct action." *Wildfire Issue* 1. April 2015. Retrieved from https://wildfire.noblogs.org/files/2015/04/wildfire-1.pdf

Swan, P. (2016). "Joshua Scolman, having a really hard time in solitary." *Stranded Friends*. August, 2016. Retrieved from https://needsfriendsnow.blogspot.com/2016/08/joshua-scolman-having-really-hard-time.html

Taylor, K-Y. (2016). *From #BlackLivesMatter to black liberation*. Chicago, IL: Haymarket Books.

Thompson, H. A. (2017). "What happened at Vaughn prison?" *Jacobin*. February 2, 2017. Retrieved from https://www.jacobinmag.com/2017/02/vaughn-prison-hostage-attica-uprising/

The Thread. (2016). "Episode 1: Prison organizing, fighting poverty, and electoral politics." *DefeatMassIncarceration.com*. June 1, 2016. Retrieved from http://www.defeatmassincarceration.com/uploads/1/9/3/5/19356953/the_thread_ep1_transcript_6-1-16.pdf

Turk, B. (2016a). "Free Alabama movement may day work stoppage interview." *Truth-Out*. May 27, 2016. Retrieved from http://www.truth-out.org/speakout/item/36216-free-alabama-movement-may-day-work-stoppage-interview

Turk, B. (2016b). "Power on the inside: Why incarcerated lives matter to the black lives matter movement." *[zine]* Retrieved from https://itsgoingdown.org/power-inside-incarcerated- lives-matter-black-lives-matter-movement/

Turk, B. (2016c). "Dying to live hunger strikers kept on the brink of death by retaliatory DOC." *Dying to Live*. August 22, 2016. Retrieved from https://solitarytorture.blogspot.com/2016/08/dying-to-live-hunger-strikers-kept-on.html

Wynter, S. (2003). "Unsettling the coloniality of being/power/truth/freedom: Towards the human, after man, its overrepresentation – An argument." *The New Centennial Review*, 3(3), 257–337.

5. *From Prison Abolition to Transformative Justice*

LAURA MAGNANI

It should be enough, in arguing for prison abolition, to demonstrate that the prison system does not work. Prison does not make us safe, nor does it rehabilitate prisoners or avenge wrong doing. The 60–80% recidivism rates around the country attest to prison failure (https://www.nij.gov/topics/corrections/recidivism/Pages/welcome.aspx). In fact, an incarcerated person becomes acculturated to a system of violence and domination, which infantilizes its subjects and offers little preparation for life on the outside.

Aside from the prison system's failure, there is the moral bankruptcy of a setting that justifies violence in the name of punishment, engages in sophisticated forms of racial profiling and racial segregation, and allows itself to become—for all practical purposes—a hate factory. This social and psychological injury does not stop at the gates. All people coming into contact with the prison system are damaged: family members, workers at the facility, children of incarcerated parents, and people who are victims of crimes. All of these parties are "doing time." To justify the prison system as it currently operates is to legitimize a system of extreme personal violence and alienation. Prisons force us to normalize inhumane conditions and to normalize the social and psychological damage done to families. Prison legitimates the beatings and "justifiable homicides" law enforcement perpetrate frequently, compromising our humanity.

As I sit in my office today, at the American Friends Service Committee, I am receiving word that a prisoner granted parole after 30 years, who had no write-ups inside prison during his tenure, was "detained" at release based on an outstanding warrant. The warrant was for a misdemeanor forgery charge dating back 30 years. The local jurisdiction has set bail at $100,000 for this misdemeanor after the man has served more time in prison than his offense warranted (misdemeanors carry a maximum of one year). When governments are given absolute power over people there is a constant danger of the abuse of that power. Citizens pay taxes for a criminal justice system that often abuses its power in the name of "justice" by violating citizens' humanity and dignity. This scenario is played out again and again daily. Whenever courts require the release of a person held too long, law enforcement challenges the order. Though the criminal justice system purports to be guided by the rule of law, enforcers too often see themselves as above the law, as is frequently demonstrated. In 1971, the American Friends Service Committee issued a policy statement which reads as follows:

> We submit that the basic evils of imprisonment are that it denies autonomy, degrades dignity, impairs or destroys self-reliance, inculcates authoritarian values, minimizes the likelihood of beneficial interaction with one's peers, fractures family ties, destroys the family's economic stability, and prejudices the prisoner's future prospects for any improvement in his economic and social status. It does all these things whether or not the buildings are antiseptic or dirty, the aroma that of fresh bread or stale urine, the sleeping accommodation a plank or an inner-spring mattress. (American Friends Service Committee, 1971 p. 33)

The point is that the prison system stands on such a corrupt foundation in terms of its purposes and is carried out through the raw exercise of legitimized power—one person over another—that fixing it is quite impossible. Indeed, even as we are watching dramatic decreases in prison populations around the country, budgets for "corrections" departments are not shrinking. Instead, according to the Legislative Analyst's office, the price of incarcerating a prisoner has risen in California by about 45% since 2011. The average per prisoner cost in 2016–2017 is $71,000/year (http://www.lao.ca.gov/PolicyAreas/CJ/6_cj_inmatecost). Of that amount, less than $5000 goes to rehabilitation, education, and vocational training. The vast majority of the investment goes to security.

The vested interests make up what is called the Prison Industrial Complex (PIC). The PIC is defined by the national organization Critical Resistance as follows:

> A term we use to describe the overlapping interests of government and industry that use surveillance, policing, and imprisonment as solutions to economic, social and political problems. Through its reach and impact, the PIC helps and maintains the authority of people who get their power through racial, economic and other privileges. There are many ways this power is collected and maintained through the PIC, including creating mass media images that keep alive stereotypes of people of color, poor people, queer people, immigrants, youth, and other oppressed communities as criminal, delinquent, or deviant. This power is also maintained by earning huge profits for private companies that deal with prisons and police

> forces; helping earn political gains for "tough on crime" politicians; increasing the influence of prison guard and police unions; and eliminating social and political dissent by oppressed communities that make demands for self-determination and reorganization of power in the US. (Critical Resistance, 2017)

Whenever there are such complex vested interests, dismantling the prison system becomes problematic. There are many stakeholders. Many towns feel dependent on a prison industry, even as the industry pits community members against each other destroying the possibilities for real community solidarity. Even as people are released from prisons, the for-profit sector has found ways to capitalize on their release by garnering contracts for ankle bracelets, re-entry facilities, or various new forms of surveillance. So rather than disappearing from inmates lives, the industry simply puts on new clothes.

Coalitions in California expressly trying to reduce the prison population and move us away from incarceration have concluded that only if prisons are closed will reducing the population save money and actually shrink the system. However, there are special interests that work against such a strategy including lawmakers afraid of public reaction and victims' rights groups. The California prison guard's union, California Correctional Peace Officers Association, spent $7.4 million dollars in support of proposition 66 which sped up the death penalty process in California (State of California, 2017). Their annual spending on a variety of issues has made them one of the largest political contributors in the state. Still, there are a number of key legislators who are tied to increasing the prison budget year after year as the numbers of people kept inside decreases.

Prison abolition is necessary because perpetuating the rationalizations that underlie the system—the right to use lethal force against prisoners, the presumed efficacy of punishment, permission to treat fellow human beings as sub-human and deserving of disrespect and demonization—means that we will continue to reap what we sew. We have to start sewing something different.

The Norway Model

Not all countries treat people who have committed crimes so inhumanely. Scandinavian countries have long experimented with more positive approaches and see a person sent to them as someone who made a mistake and needs helps getting integrated back into the community. In Norway, the attitude is that people who have committed crimes have lost their freedom but should not also lose their dignity. Everyone has a job or an educational assignment. Each person has their own room. There are common areas for socializing, cooking meals, and recreating. As much as possible, the environment mimics life on the outside. Most people are there for less than a year and during that time acquire skills, get help with medical and mental health issues, and are treated with respect by staff. Staff undergo two years of training to determine if they are a good fit for this service. Rather than taking away their individuality, as the U.S. does in its prisons, Norway looks for ways for people to live productively as the person they already are. Hoping to promote this model to different jurisdictions in the U.S., the Berkeley-based Prison Law Office, in partnership with The University of California Criminal Justice and Health Consortium, initiated and funded a project to take corrections officials, legislators, and administrators from various states to Norway to see the system for themselves. Delegations apply and are accepted for the tours based on their openness to make changes when they return, and whether their delegation includes the people with authority to make the changes (Prison Law Office, 2016).

As a Board member of the Prison Law Office, I have watched this project unfold, seen the lessons learned, and helped to monitor the results. It is a creative and inspiring approach to reform. It would not constitute prison abolition because each jurisdiction decides for itself which elements to incorporate into its carceral system. What can be expected is positive reductions in recidivism as some people are treated more humanely and more programming is made available. Some state officials who have visited Norway are coming back with ideas of their own about how to transform their systems. Clearly, a more humane approach will improve the lives of those given access to the new programs. But, if the apparatus of imprisonment remains in place in those states, the chances of the carceral mindset dominating and re-asserting itself are strong.

Re-thinking Policing

Government's role in policing is one of the hardest things for people to critically examine, because of the assumption that we all need protection from dangerous people. Just as with the military, people cannot imagine a state or local jurisdiction free from armed police forces to "protect us." What goes unexamined is how effective this protection is and who most benefits from it. In communities of color, the decision to call the police is weighed very differently than in Anglo-European communities where people trust that they will be made safer. Often communities of color are put in greater danger when they call in armed personnel whether for a domestic altercation, a break in, or an actual assault. The reason is communities of color are themselves seen as the likely criminals and when victimized are treated with suspicion and distrust.

Black Lives Matter came into existence because day after day, all over the country, African American men were being killed by the police in simple traffic stops, because they reached into a pocket, because they failed to follow an order, or because they fled a situation. Who gave the police unlimited rights to execute people who had never even been charged with a crime, much less convicted? These incidents are not new, they have just come to light because of cell phones and body cameras. Zimring's (2017) new book breaks down the difficulty in determining the exact number of police killings per year. After comparing different sources, he asserts that the research done by The Guardian newspaper is the most reliable, coming in at approximately twice the number of killings reported by law enforcement itself. In 2015, the number including both shootings and deaths by other devices was 1134 (Zimring, 2017 p. 35). Of those deaths, 26.1% were African Americans at a time when Blacks made up 12.2% of the population of the U.S. (Zimring, 2017 p. 35). In fact, Black and First Nations peoples were killed at more than twice their proportional representation in the population. White Non-Hispanics were killed at a rate slightly below their proportional representation in the population, 51.9%, compared to 55.7% (Zimring, 2017 p. 45). According to the Washington post (another source cited by Zimring as reliable for these statistics), 232 African Americans were killed by the police in 2016 (Tate et al., 2016).

What is important about these numbers is the picture they paint of what police forces do with the power they are given by society and how society's attitudes about race play out. Should we be giving this kind of power to anyone while the realities of racism continue unaddressed? It is worth noting that such power does not only manifest in one-on-one police shootings, but also in the increasingly militaristic training given to police to carry out their duties. Police armed with automatic weapons, tanks, drones and other military weaponry, and trained to shoot to kill rather than to de-escalate situations increase the likelihood of fatalities and raise the stakes with respect to the justification of authority vested in these forces.

In this chapter, I am not trying to make the case for eliminating the police, but I am trying to make the case, as much as one can in one chapter, for dismantling prisons, also known commonly as prison abolition. Moreover, I am working to dismantle the whole punitive justice system grounded in punishment, domination and control, of which the police play a significant part. I want to start the conversation on better ways to protect ourselves without resorting to the lethal force of either public or private security forces. Community groups organizing against Urban Shield, for instance, point out that the majority of funding that could be supporting emergency preparedness in the San Francisco Bay Area has been poured into increasing the militarization of local law enforcement. This broad coalition of over 20 grassroots, social justice, and faith-based organizations are advocating holistic and sustainable approaches to safety and to natural disasters by providing adequate health care, mental health care, food security, job training, affordable housing, and fully funded public schools. One might argue that addressing the underlying causes of street crime is not helping someone who is actually being assaulted. But providing people with jobs, adequate housing, and healthcare will cut down on the instances of victimization and make people less desperate. Investing in substance abuse treatment and mental health care will have similar results.

The real aim of this coalition is to train communities in emergency responses that are neighborhood based and which prioritize problem solving and positive intervention rather than violence and alienation. Trainings have been developed by different groups in response to the need. For example, Occupy Oakland, through its Medics Committee, came together as volunteer lay health workers to teach each other how to respond to medical emergencies. The refusal of police to call an ambulance for Oscar Grant for 20 minutes as he lay fatally wounded clarified the need for alternatives and drove the creation of these trainings (Oakland Power Projects, 2017).

Clearly such trainings and accompanying services would require a reordering of priorities so that resources are available to fund schools, after school programs, provide health care, etc. As long as we continue to delegate responses to organizations primarily trained in the use of force the levels of alienation will persist and grow. The California Nurses Association, in a recent letter to the Alameda County Board of Supervisors said:

> We strongly support the development, support, and expansion of true Emergency Preparedness programming in Alameda County. We are distressed to learn that our Board of Supervisors plans on allocating five of the $6 Million dollars granted by UASI Urban Shield, while not spending a single dollar on many of the emergency preparedness goals, such as Goal 1: Planning and Risk Management, Goal 5: Medical and Public Health, Goal 6: Emergency Planning and Community Preparedness, or Goal 7: Recovery.
>
> We do not support programs that train first responders and law enforcement officials to see the people who live in our communities as their greatest threat. We do not support increasing the use of militarized weaponry and tactics in everyday law enforcement. These training exercises perpetuate racist and xenophobic stereotypes and increase trauma in communities already suffering under the massive number of police killings, militarized SWAT raids and sweeps, and surveillance technologies and are further eroding already fragile community/police relationships. This decreases public safety, destabilizes communities, and puts more cops at risk. (http://stopurbanshield.org/wp-content/uploads/2017/04/CNASUSLetter.pdf)

Transforming the Carceral System

What would it look like if the one-size-fits-all prison system, also known as the carceral system, were abandoned and other mechanisms employed when wrong doing occurred? The truth is the answers have been at work in some cultures for hundreds, maybe thousands of years. Most have been pioneered by indigenous peoples and some have been re-invented to fit settings in U.S. cities and rural areas. The model has often been called "restorative justice" and has at its core the intention of wholeness and healing of all parties rather than violence and punishment. However, the term "restorative justice" has come into question, because it presumes that there is something to be restored whether that is a certain level of functionality, a more level playing field, or a true sense of community around the people affected. One significant difference between indigenous cultures and the dominant culture in the U.S. is that tribal cultures have the potential for real community, whereas there are many cultures and groupings within the United States that arise to fill a variety of needs, some healthy and some harmful. Currently, there is much evidence of xenophobic, anti-Semitic, racially hateful groups finding voice and acting out, often violently. It would be naïve to suggest that all "communities" are positive. The transformative processes of which I speak are about the common good—the good of all—and ways to enhance and grow toward that goal.

The possibility of such a radical re-orientation is remote. Instead, it is likely to become a reality in a more piecemeal form, reintroducing the danger that the change will bring some new reforms while continuing to prop up the existing system. This is already happening in a number of jurisdictions where elements are added onto the punishment system in the name of restorative justice, but are in fact just another punishment. Restitution is now commonly added to people's prison sentence so that people are expected to pay restitution to victims and, if they are released from prison, are released with huge debts to pay. This comes on top of the fact that few people coming out of prison can find jobs to support themselves and their families. The process has become a kind of debtors' prison in reverse. Restitution by itself could be a good concept. A number of European countries automatically compensate victims of crime to aid in their healing process. However, their systems are not dependent on the defendant assuming the financial burden. By the state assuming that responsibility, the state is sharing in the responsibility for the harm that has occurred—an important element of transformative justice.

The shift to this model asks a different question in resolving wrong doing. The question is "How do we heal the harm?" not "How do we punish the criminal?". The current system assumes that there are individual actors with individual culpability, so the resolution is between perpetrator and victim. Transformative (or restorative) Justice takes into account three factors: the person harmed, the person who did the harm, the context around the event or the society at large. Incidents do not happen in a vacuum. In the carceral system, the role of the state is to catch, try, and punish the perpetrator. The victim or survivor is pushed to the side and the state takes the role of the survivor. If the actual survivor has a role it is to support the case against the defendant. There is no room for healing or for bringing the parties together.

In "restorative justice," "community justice," "transformative justice"—whatever term we like best—the vision is to build a society which honors individual dignity and the centrality of relationships which give meaning to our lives. The cycle of despair concerning crime, fed by anger and fear, can become a cycle of hope when we create processes in which every participant is valued and every voice (i.e., the victim, the community, the offender) are heard with respect to expressing pain, anger, fear, remorse, anguish or hope. "There is no blueprint for a restorative response to crime. Each community must create its own vision and its own array of responses that take advantage of its unique resources and circumstances and are guided by restorative values" (Pranis, 1997).

Learning from the experiences of so many indigenous cultures around the world, there are increasing numbers of experiments in alternative forms of justice being tried around the U.S. The state of Minnesota was one of the first to have an office with a full-time staff person devoted to restorative justice practices. Aided by the Minnesota Restorative Justice Initiative, restorative practices were tried in a variety of settings with both juveniles and adults. The Minnesota Department of Corrections website still describes some restorative principles, but clearly stays within the model of individual responsibility falling to the perpetrator.

It is still rare for transformative practices to replace the punitive model of justice. The closest to replacing the punitive of justice happened in the Oakland schools where disciplinary systems were actually replaced with circle processes. When an incident occurred, instead of sending a student to the office for punishment, usually resulting in suspension or expulsion, the students sat down in a circle to talk about what happened, how it impacted each person, and what could be done to resolve the conflict. Often overlooked issues, like what was happening to students at home or in their outside lives, provided the key to the cause of their acting out. Often times students just needed to be listened to. Restorative Justice for Oakland Youth (RJOY) has garnered a national reputation for its pioneering restorative work. Under their influence, the Oakland Unified School District was able to change its Zero Tolerance Disciplinary Policies.

Results

In Oakland schools using Restorative Justice, suspensions of African American students decreased by 40% in one year to 420 students. Conflicts were resolved successfully in over 76% of the 500 harm circles that were held (Jain et al., 2014 p. 4). Graduation rates in schools using restorative justice practices saw an increase in graduation rates of 60% between 2011 and 2014 as opposed to 7% in schools not using Restorative Justice (Jain et al., 2014 p. 6). Seventy percent of staff reported that restorative practices were helping to improve the school climate at their school (Jain et al., 2014 pp. iv–vi).

The Restorative Justice Project of the organization Impact Justice is working in a number of locations in California as well as 10 jurisdictions across the country training community based organizations in both Circle Process and Restorative Community Conference (RCC) in pre-booking diversion models for youth accused of crime. They are paying special attention to the importance of culturally appropriate methods that are victim oriented. In Alameda County, the recidivism rates for youth receiving restorative justice services is half of that for youth handled only through the legal system (Impact Justice, 2016).

The University of Wisconsin Population Health Institute conducted a study of restorative justice programs in its state. The definition of such programs used in the report varied widely. The programs could occur throughout the criminal justice process, from pre-arrest to post-sentence, in prisons, therapeutic facilities, and communities. They found strong evidence that restorative justice reduces recidivism. Victims who participated had greater levels of satisfaction with the justice process. Researchers also found that the use of restorative justice conferences reduced post-traumatic stress symptoms among participants ("What Works for Health," 2010, http://whatworksforhealth.wisc.edu/program.php?tl=20&12=113&t3=101&id=494).

The track record for transformational programs is growing. The question is whether these isolated experiments can actually rise to the level of producing systemic change. Over and over, we have seen wonderful programs get funded for a few years, have positive evaluations, and then disappear as the funding disappears. Prying funding loose from entrenched criminal justice systems has been daunting. In California, when the U.S. Supreme Court required the state to reduce its prison population, and when multiple ballot measures de-criminalized various offenses, there was hope that money could be re-directed to community programs. Nevertheless, Sheriff Departments and other law enforcement entities have gobbled up the lion's share of these monies to build more facilities, even as they re-purpose the facilities as mental health units or program-oriented jails. Transformative Justice is not a slightly cleaner, prettier jail, as the AFSC policy statement at the beginning of this chapter outlines. A recent proposal for a Youth Leadership Academy presented the same dilemma. We want youth to have better options than simply being housed in traditional lock ups and yet, at the end of the day, this proposal was a veiled way of expanding the number of prisons the state already possesses (Davis, 2017).

Is it possible to build a parallel system that could demonstrate truly healing methodologies? Could this be done without expanding the net of the criminal justice system, where the people sent to the parallel system were people who never would have found their way to prison in the first place? Would a more de-centralized approach, with a range of options to choose from be more realistic as well as more creative? While new programs are always being required to demonstrate their effectiveness, could the carceral state be required to provide evidence-based data on its effectiveness? Programs with a positive track records should be the ones funded by taxpayer dollars.

References

American Friends Service Committee. (1971). *Struggle for Justice: A Report on Crime and Punishment in America.* New York, NY: Hill and Wang.

Critical Resistance. (2017). *What Is the PIC? What Is Abolition?* Retrieved May 31, 2017, from http://criticalresistance.org/about/not-so-common-language/

Davis, C. (2017). *People Are Calling out This Educational Academy.* Retrieved May 31, 2017, from https://www.attn.com/stories/14530/california-leadership-academy-prison

Impact Justice. (2016). *Restorative Justice Project.* Retrieved May 31, 2017, from http://impactjustice.org/restorative-justice-project/

Jain, S., H. Bassey, M.A. Brown, & P. Kalra. (2014). *Restorative Justice in Oakland Schools Impacts and Implementation.* Oakland, CA: Oakland Unified School District.

Oakland Power Projects—*Health Resources.* (2017). Retrieved May 31, 2017, from http://criticalresistance.org/opphealthresources/

Prison Law Office. (2016). *The US-European Criminal Justice Innovation Program: 2015–16 Program Evaluation.*

Pranis, K. (1997). "The Minnesota Restorative Justice Initiative: A Model Experience." *The Crime Victims Report,* 1(2).

State of California, Secretary of State. (February 7, 2017). *Ballot Measure Total Contributions –2016.* Retrieved from http://www.sos.ca.gov/campaign-lobbying/cal-access-resources/measure-contributions/proposition-66-death-penalty-procedures-initiative-statute/

Tate, J., J. Jenkins, & S. Rich. (2016). "Fatal Force." *The Washington Post.* http://m.huffpost.com/us/entry/us_577da633e4b0c590f7e7fb17)

What Works for Health: Policies and Programs to Improve Wisconsin's Health. (2010). "Restorative Justice in the Criminal Justice System." *University of Wisconsin Population Health Institute: School of Medicine and Public Health.* http://whatworksforhealth.wisc.edu/program.php?tl=20&12=113&t3=101&id=494

Zimring, F. E. (2017). *When Police Kill.* Cambridge, MA: Harvard University Press.

6. *An Anarchist Criminology for Understanding Environmental Degradation*

MARK SEIS

Introduction

The obvious role of criminology in combatting environmental degradation and crime has been through advocating for tougher environmental laws, comprehensive enforcement, and rigorous prosecution (Clifford and Edwards, 2012). Most environmental crime has been viewed from the lens of conflict/Marxist criminology (Lynch and Michalowski, 2006). From this perspective, owners of capital use their financial influence and political power to manipulate, undermine, and violate environmental legislative mandates to maximize profit. The private interests of capital are not neutral and neither are the interests of the state. The state supports the economic growth objectives of the capitalist class yet is entrusted with maintaining the public welfare. The compromise of appeasing the capitalist class while protecting the public welfare often results in ineffective regulatory agencies. In short, regulatory agencies are often captured by endless compromise between the interest of capital and the interests of the public (Anderson, 1982; Barnett 1994; Frank and Lombness, 1988; Seis 2001). Heads of industry or industry proponents are often appointed by the reigning political administration to oversee regulatory agencies, which amounts to the industry attempting to regulate itself while preserving the public interest—witness Representative Scott Pruitt, a fierce proponent of oil and gas and fierce opponent of the Environmental Protection Agency (EPA) being appointed to head the agency. A pro-business executive branch of government and congress are not going to provide the necessary funding and tools to create a strong environmental crime enforcement presence. Challenging the status quo of consumer capitalism and its right to exploit for those ends will always result in politicized and compromised protections for environmental safety. The relentless struggle between the contradictions of consumer capitalism and efforts to maintain a clean and healthy environment is irreconcilable (Seis, 2001). The insatiable need for capitalist economies to endlessly grow violates the most basic laws of nature. Infinite growth on a finite planet is simply not possible. The effort to regulate the voracious appetite of growth based capitalism with mandated increments of acceptable levels of compromised environmental degradation amounts to a steady normalized decline in the health of our environment (e.g., air and water pollution, soil erosion, species extinction, climate change, toxic food and landscapes, and loss of overall biodiversity). More law and regulation will not resolve the contradiction of a lifestyle based on crass consumerism and endless growth.

Given the fundamental contradiction of consumer capitalism and environmental health, it behooves us to think about the problem of environmental degradation from a different cultural perspective. Some of the most environmentally sustainable cultures in human history were cultures without governments or formalized legal structures.

This chapter examines our environmental crisis from the perspective of cultural construction. In other words, how does culture either normalize environmental degradation or make environmental degradation appear insane? In order to address this problem, this chapter is divided into three sections. First, it is necessary to understand the counter-ecological nature of our culture and why it cannot be remedied through legal means. Second, we will examine some of the cultural characteristics of successful Indigenous sustainable cultures. Finally, we will survey current ideas regarding building sustainable communities with relocalization efforts.

Bad Culture and the Fallacy of the Law Solution

The practice of sedentary agriculture marks a major shift in humankind's relationship to the land. Sedentary agriculture led to major alterations in ecosystems in order to grow crops and pasture animals, and it led to major changes in human social organization and even our physical evolution (Glendinning, 1994; Gowdy, 1998; Jensen, 2016; Lieberman, 2013; Manicardi, 2012; Oelschlaeger, 1991; Ponting, 1991; Shepard, 1998; Wells 2010; Zerzan, 1994). Sedentary agricultural societies are also associated with the birth of civilization, creating a binary between civilized and so called "primitive cultures." Sedentary agriculture also marks the beginning of our alienation from the natural world. As Ponting suggests, agriculture "involves replacing the natural system with an artificial one..." (1991, p. 33). Agriculture requires the binary split between tame and wild, pitting humans against all aspects of nature that interfere with our ability to produce our sustenance (i.e., insects, weeds, and other competitor species) (Oelschlaeger, 1991; Ponting 1991; Shepard, 1998; Wells 2010). Ponting writes:

> Agriculture is most definitely not an easier option than gathering and hunting. It requires far more effort in clearing land, sowing, tending and harvesting crops and in looking after domesticated animals. It does not necessarily provide more nutritious food, nor does it offer greater security because it selects and depends on a far smaller range of plants and animals. (1991, p. 41)

Prior to agriculture, humans roamed the land freely, foraging from the great earth garden without much thought of scarcity. Gathering and hunting "was without doubt the most successful and flexible way of life adopted by humans and the one that caused the least damage to natural ecosystems" (Ponting, 1991, p. 18). In sum, agriculture forces humankind to leave the garden and begin the project of reconstructing the world to serve human needs and wants (Glendinning, 1994; Gowdy, 1998; Jensen, 2016; Lieberman, 2013; Manicardi, 2012; Oelschlaeger, 1991; Ponting, 1991; Shepard, 1998; Wells 2010; Zerzan, 1994).

Despite the periodic famines that followed agriculture, population growth increased in the Neolithic villages to levels unknown to hunting and gathering humans (Wells, 2010). Along with population growth came serious alterations in landscapes through irrigation and deforestation. Neolithic villages gave way to cities and hierarchically organized governments fostering and protecting social systems of stratification. The ability of agriculture to produce surplus food led to a division of labor that over time became stratified based on its ability to serve the larger ambitions of hierarchically organized institutions of power (Glendinning, 1994; Jensen, 2016; Lieberman, 2013; Manicardi, 2012; Oelschlaeger, 1991; Ponting, 1991; Shepard, 1998; Wells 2010; Zerzan, 1994). The life of toil implicit in socially stratified societies led to salvation based monotheistic religions, militarism, and patriarchal forms of power and domination. With the rise of the city-state, women's roles declined quickly to mothers of males and servants of the patriarchal family (Manicardi, 2012). All of these changes in post hunting and gathering cultures are viewed as progress, a mythical concept that presupposes we are destined to live in some postlapsarian techno-wonder-world free from the perceived tyranny of nature.

To make a long and fascinating history told superbly by the people cited here short, sedentary agriculture led to an increasing control over nature and humans through fostering the rise of slavery, feudalism, and capitalism. The domination of nature and humans is the product of a radical shift in how we produced our food. Whatever the disputed initial causes of this change in our food producing behavior were, we are now confronted with a consumer based industrial culture that perceives human beings outside of nature as the supreme beings of this planet (Jensen, 2016). Hence, the entire edifice of consumer capitalism is based on the premise that nature is a gigantic resource destined for human consumption. The entire political and legal apparatus is designed to facilitate the extraction of resources to serve the postlapsarian-techno-wonder-world ambitions of humankind. Therefore, to rely on the promulgation of law, grounded in the values of human supremacism and consumer capitalism, as a tool to curtail and preclude further environmental degradation is ecocidal.

Consumer capitalism coupled with the ideological belief of human supremacism has produced a civilization that has exceeded the carrying capacity of our landbase as demonstrated by our ability to change the climate of the earth and the chemistry of the oceans, drive multiple species to extinction, and taint the air, water, and land with chemicals unknown to the natural world. Any way you slice it, consumer capitalism guided by the ethos of human supremacism is a force to be reckoned with, and no legal system operating within the confines of consumer capitalism and the ethos of human supremacism will be able to change the suicidal trajectory of pursuing unlimited growth on a finite planet.

The anarchist Peter Kropotkin argued that "law is the product of modern times. For ages and ages mankind lived without any written law…human relations were simply regulated by customs, habits and usages, made sacred by constant repetition and acquired by each person in childhood" (2002, p. 201). According to Kropotkin, the social nature of humans based on our need for affirmation is a much greater deterrent to bad behavior than is threat of punishment from law. The basis of written law has its origins, according to Kropotkin, in the "protection of property, protection of persons, protection of government" (2002, p. 212). With respect to property, Kropotkin saw the law as a way to "secure to certain other people that portion of the produce which they have stolen either from the producer or from society as a whole" (2002, p. 212). Kropotkin's point here is to illustrate how the capitalist class usurps public resources for their own economic gain just as they steal wealth produced by workers by paying them wages lower than the value of what they produce. Property law is designed to assure those who have capital maintain their privileged status by protecting their right to pilfer individual workers and public resources. There is no greater evidence of this than the growing gulf between rich and poor and the relentless theft of public land resources by corporations whether it be through mining, logging, or oil and gas extraction.

With respect to the protection of government, the mission of law is obviously to protect by "legitimate" force the privileges of the upper classes who are in possession of the reins of government (Kropotkin, 2002, p. 214). Kropotkin argues that the majority of "laws on taxes, excise duties, the organization of ministerial departments and their offices, of the army, the police... have no other end than to maintain...the administrative machine...[which] in its turn serves almost entirely to protect the privileges of the possessing class" (2002, p. 214). And regarding the purpose of law as protecting protect persons from other persons, Kropotkin notes that the majority of crimes against persons are the result of extremely stratified societies whereby "such crimes are instigated by the desire to obtain possession of someone's wealth" (2002, p. 214). If law was a deterrent to bad behavior, then modern nation-states should have little to no crime.

As anarchists have been demonstrating for centuries, the law within the confines of a capitalist and human supremacist culture has done very little to discourage bad behavior, but its real efficacy has been in the preservation of inequality and protecting the right of the upper classes to pilfer public resources and to degrade the environment for personal profit. What is required to deal with our present course of ecocide is to reimagine a different relationship with the natural world. The environmental crisis is a cultural crisis and requires a change in our cultural ethos as well as our social construction of economy, governance, and relationship.

Key Characteristics of Sustainable Cultures

Sustainable cultures are those that connect people to landbases in such a way that cultural and economic practices can be engaged in indefinitely without degradation to any particular aspect of the landbase. When viewing historically the multitude of Indigenous people who lived in almost every climate and bioregion on the earth, the overall majority of them left behind viable, healthy ecosystems before being conquered by so called "civilized" people (Ponting, 1991). In fact, the justification by "civilized" people for stealing Indigenous peoples' land was that they were not using the land in the "proper way." The Catholic Church coined the term the "Doctrine of Discovery" to justify the conquest and theft of Indigenous lands around the world. Those Indigenous cultures who maintained hunting/gathering lifestyles with minimum reliance on agriculture tended to leave few traces of their sustainable way of life.

Unlike "civilized" agricultural people, Indigenous people viewed nature as home. Indigenous means first people of a particular region. As noted earlier, one of the greatest shifts in consciousness due to our reliance on agriculture was the creation of the tame/wild binary. For agriculturalists, nature was wild and needed to be tamed, cleared of impediments to farming. There was no binary for Indigenous people, nature was not wild it was home. Nature was viewed as a community of interdependent life forms of which humans were just one facet of the landscape (Oelschlaeger, 1991; Ponting, 1991; Shepard, 1998). Such conceptions of nature are very difficult for modern people who have become frightened by the thought of wild landscapes. Commercial media reinforces just how scary the woods can be (i.e., bears, wolves, coyotes, etc.) and why people need automobiles to escape it quickly, seeking the safety of paved manicured landscapes.

Indigenous sustainable cultures viewed nature as alive. Therefore, nature confronts Indigenous people with multiple subjectivities, and it is incumbent upon sustainable cultures to form relationships with all of them. Trees, plants, and animals all have intrinsic value and all have a subjective existence different from humans but no less significant, which makes the whole of nature sacred. The vast repertoire of knowledge obtained by Indigenous sustainable cultures regarding plants' medicinal and edible uses baffles many scientists today (Buhner, 2006). Divinity was everywhere, thus all things required respect and awareness of our interdependence on all aspects of the landbase. The role of the mature adult in Indigenous sustainable cultures is to enter into relationship with the other. "Civilized" people, occupy landscapes and dominate or exterminate the other based on its service to human supremacism (Jensen, 2016). To the "civilized," nature is viewed as a utility for meeting the unlimited needs of human beings. It is the exception for "civilized" people to recognize intrinsic value in the multiple subjectivities of nature (Oelschlaeger, 1991; Shepard, 1998).

Time was synchronous rather than diachronic, which means most Indigenous sustainable cultures lived in the eternal present. Life was a series of sacred cycles like the seasons of the year, which repeated, affirming the eternal present of nature. Life itself was a cycle of renewal and death of which we are all participants. Indigenous cultures celebrated the eternal cycles of life with seasonal ceremonies and celebrations commemorating the journey that all life is destined to follow (Oelschlaeger, 1991). "Civilized" cultures live in time which is said to be headed toward the future or as I tell my students to Progressville. Progressville is the endless pursuit of a world where everything will be made easy through life-improving technologies and some day immortality will be achieved. Infantile fantasies of this sort are touted daily in contemporary culture, always promising a better life in the future, leaving no time to live in the present.

Diachronic time also moves humans out of their environment and places them on their own trajectory through written history. History is the story of humans and their endeavors outside of nature. As Neil Evernden puts it, rather than seeking meaning in nature "man becomes the measure of all, for he now believes himself to be all that is important. Once meaning is confiscated by a single source, the world is devalued, transformed into an empty vessel containing material for human use" (1999, p. 85). Such a perspective may be why contemporary cultures are filled with such high rates of suicide, depression, and existential angst. To think that humans are the apex of life is to ignore a vast, intelligent, and incredibly complex world.

Another common practice among Indigenous sustainable cultures was totemism. As Max Oelschlaeger suggests "the identification of a hunting-gathering clan with a species of plant or animal, supports the conjecture that Paleolithic people believed themselves to be one with nature" (1991, p. 12). While the clan structure was devised to prevent incest, it also was a reflection of a shared sense of community with the other occupants of the landbase community. The animals chosen to represent clans had specific virtues, which were sources of pride for those lucky enough to be associated with them through their clan affiliation. It is somewhat interesting that this practice still lingers in our contemporary world in the form of mascots. Unfortunately, most of the mascots chosen by civilized people are animals that are endangered or on the verge of extinction by civilized human land practices (i.e., Grizzly Bears, Wolves, Wolverines, Tigers, etc.).

Another major feature of sustainable Indigenous cultures is the employment of democratic forms of technology which manifest more democratic social forms of engagement. Lewis Mumford (1967) referred to the difference between Paleolithic and post-Neolithic cultures as one of democratic technics versus authoritarian technics. Mumford writes that democratic technics "had the security that comes from petty operations under the direct control of the participants, following a customary pattern in a familiar environment" (1967, p. 237). Sustainable cultures possessing technologies given freely by nature and accessible to all leads to what Mumford called "[t]he spinal principle of democracy [which] is the perception that the traits and needs and interests that all men share have a superior claim to those put forward by any special organization, institution or group" (1967, p. 236). Authoritarian technics are complex specialized technologies generally designed and managed by specific organizations, institutions, or states making it "much easier to wipe out democracy by an institutional arrangement that gives authority only to those at the apex of social hierarchy" (Mumford, 1967, p. 236). When the level of technology is democratically accessible to all, and when all people face-to-face decide that preservation of their landbases is imperative to present and future generations, then "[u]under democratic technics the only occupation that demanded a lifetime's attention was that of becoming a full human being…" (Mumford, 1967, p. 238). Authoritarian technics, on the other hand, "in its original servile form did not share these life-enhancing propensities: it centered, not on the worker and his life, but on the product, the system of production, and the material or pecuniary gains therefrom…the megamachine worked for speed, uniformity, standardization, quantification" (Mumford, 1967, pp. 238–239).

It is undeniable that the more complex the technology the more insidious and domineering the social forms of control, and the more alienated we become from the landbases we occupy. In post-modern consumer capitalism, most people have no idea where their water, food, clothing, energy, materials for domiciles, and materials for transportation originate. In fact, most people are conditioned to not care. So, why would we expect people to care about destructive mining, logging, oil and gas production, and destructive industrial agricultural practices when they are oblivious to its impact on "other" humans and nonhumans? Consumer capitalism disguises the entire regime of production from beginning to end. The consumer participates only insofar as shopping for the lowest prices, oblivious to the conditions of how commodities are produced and made.

This kind of alienated production was completely incomprehensible to sustainable cultures who were aware of all interactions with their landbase. Everyone knew where their water, food, clothing, and material for their domiciles came from. This constant interaction with land was reinforced in myths and stories told around campfires used to teach young people their obligations of reciprocity with their biotic communities. Scholars like Joseph Campbell and Mircea Eliade spent countless hours analyzing the significance of mythic consciousness and its role in grounding its participants in the divine interconnection between people and nature. There were myths and stories about the relationship between people and plants, people and animals, and people and sacred landmarks. With these myths and stories came morals and lessons about exploitation and overuse of resources and most importantly about reciprocal relationships. Contemporary culture offers but few examples of these types of stories that bind humans to nature and their particular landbases. In my small town, we have River Days, Snowdown, Meltdown, and an Apple Festival. These events are at least acknowledgments of the role that nature plays in our lives. However, they fall far short of elaborate stories teaching us morality, obligation, and relationship with nature.

Many readers may have two critical questions regarding what has been said thus far. Why is this guy romanticizing primitive cultures? Does he really think we can go back to living like Indigenous people with simple technologies? To answer the first, it is important to recognize that hunting/gathering sustainable Indigenous cultures have been studied for a long time and the research has consistently suggested that their cultures provided stark empirical differences in their lifestyles and beliefs as demonstrated in the literature, some of which is cited in this paper. Accusations of romanticizing Indigenous people have been leveled at researchers in order to dismiss stark cultural differences in favor of an ideology that supports the perspective that human nature is homogenously selfish and greedy despite cultural context. Such accusations are simply unfounded and lack serious knowledge of a body of literature empirically grounded.

With respect to the second question, the answer is no because our numbers are far too great, and it is impossible for us to ignore our complete dependence on our technological infrastructure. One of the most daunting aspects of our technological prowess has been our unprecedented population growth. Humans reached their first billion sometime very early in the 1800s with the estimates now being over 7.5 billion people. Twenty percent of the 7.5 billion consume a large majority of all resources with a clearly stated goal of consumer capitalism to increase the consumer appetites of as many people as possible. It is irrational to ignore the reality of our ecological crisis. Technology for all of its cleverness cannot create something from nothing. Our earth has only so much to offer and we have according to many scientists exceeded the earth's carrying capacity decades ago (Heinberg and Lerch, 2010). We are now consuming the future or committing intergenerational tyranny.

The real question is how do we respond to this crisis? How do we shrink our consumer appetites? How do we address the needs of future generations who are going to have to suffer the injustice of a severely compromised earth? It is pure ignorance to think we can continue down the same path expecting things to work out magically. The vast changes already taking place in the earth's biosphere are already severely impacting the poor and forcing many nonhuman species into extinction. To ignore this situation is immoral, and to ignore that the problem is cultural is to revel in inexcusable ignorance. Persisting in the destruction of one's habitat willingly is certainly a form of insanity. The point of this section is to recognize the fact that humans are not programmed to destroy their habitat, but cultures can be. To this end, what aspects of sustainable Indigenous culture can we introduce back into our contemporary context that may aid us in reversing our ecocidal ambitions.

Building a Sustainable Culture Through Relocalization

The role of criminology in thinking about environmental problems requires moving away from a legal solution and more toward a proactive perspective. That is, trying to combat environmental crime with more laws within a cultural framework built on growth and consumption economics is a long term losing battle from the perspective of a finite planet. The aim of anarchist criminology is to explore ways in which the culture can make environmental degradation unthinkable. To this end, what is it we can learn from past Indigenous cultures for whom the majority practiced sustainable forms of living (Ponting, 1991)?

There has been a growing body of people horrified by the prospects of peak oil and climate change who have coined the term relocalization to respond to the growing ecological crisis. The Post Carbon Institute is an organization advocating for relocalization, which they define as follows:

Relocalization is a strategy to build societies based on the local production of food, energy and goods, and the local development of currency, governance and culture. The main goals of relocalization are to increase community energy security, to strengthen local economies, and to improve environmental conditions and social equity. The relocalization strategy developed in response to the environmental, social, political and economic impacts of global over-reliance on cheap energy (www.postcarbon.org).

Relocalization is a strategy to move our consumer capitalist culture away from growth and consumption towards a vision of sustainability that starts by restructuring one community at a time. This project begins with moving away from fossil fuel infrastructure and designing communities to be self-sufficient with respect to food, transportation needs, energy, building design, local currency, and an emphasis on small business and manufacturing tailored to the needs of a local economy. The relocalization model is not new and was the predominant way towns and cities around the world took care of everyday human needs prior to the introduction of cheap fossil fuel.

Relocalization forces communities to pay attention to their bioregional surroundings by attempting to build communities within the limits of their landbases. Thus, strict attention is paid to the watershed, the climate, soil, forest, and other resources that may reside in the area. Awareness of the community surroundings dictates what is possible with respect to the types of food a community can grow. Currently, it takes anywhere from 7 to 10 calories of energy to bring one calorie of food to the table (Bomford, 2010). Food is shipped thousands of miles across countries and continents to reach our supermarkets and eventually our tables. The entire global food system is only possible due to cheap fossil fuel, which we know is not an infinite resource and remains the biggest contributor to human induced climate change. Relocalization is focused on creating community food security. According to Bomford (2010), less than one percent of the population is engaged in food production due to a heavily industrialized system that relies on cheap fossil fuel. Local food producers create jobs, reduce fossil fuel reliance and pollution, and keep money in the local economy. Local food production also leads to innovations in the production of food by encouraging composting, permaculture, organic production, and crop choices based on bioregional conditions. Local food is fresher, healthier, and more nutritious than food traveling long distances over several days of transport.

Another aspect of relocalization is to rethink the role of the automobile in our culture and transportation in general. Producing automobiles requires an immense amount of resource extraction like mining, fossil fuel energy to drive, assemble, and transport. As our cars become more electronically sophisticated, they also require more rare earth minerals. Relocalization efforts are attempting to redesign urban areas to be more bike friendly and mass transit friendly using electric powered vehicles and a rail system where possible. Another aspect of transportation is building denser urban areas with more local businesses distributed throughout the community, discouraging distant commutes to work and markets.

A further aspect of relocalization is local energy development and production. Decentralized energy grids are far more resilient and less wasteful than the mega grids and powerlines that scar our landscapes. More importantly, localized energy development seeks alternatives to fossil fuel, utilizing solar, wind, geothermal, and some forms of no dam hydro power. Building local, decentralized energy is far more efficient and democratic with respect to community involvement over choices of alternative energy applications.

Another major feature of the relocalization movement is building design. Because each locality has different access to local resources, each community's buildings should contain materials from that bioregion. Houses should contain local materials and be designed to maximize passive solar and other energy needs. It was a key feature of Indigenous cultures to use materials from the bioregions in which they lived, from living in igloos, to tepees made of buffalo hides, to mound houses, to rock houses, to timber longhouses. When communities build from their local landbases, they become aware of the environmental costs and impacts of their growth. Resources take on a whole new meaning when people are forced to confront their over exploitation. Living off your local landbase makes you aware of the costs of your chosen lifestyle.

Relocalization efforts have also focused on building communities comprised of local businesses and designing a local currency, which encourages people to buy and produce locally. Supporting local businesses keeps money in the local economy, which helps small businesses to survive and employ others. The idea is for the community to become self-sufficient before engaging in trade with other communities. There is no reason that local communities should not be able to produce local construction materials, food, energy, clothing, and other basic amenities people need. Building sustainable communities and steady state economies all boils down to scale and a conscious awareness of the carrying capacity of your landbase and the ability of the community to reciprocate and replenish that which is renewable to the landbase.

The final aspect of relocalization we will examine here is democracy and equality. It is well known fact that localalized politics are more personal and democratic. It is actually possible to contribute and communicate face-to-face with local representatives unlike state and federal legislators. More importantly, communities can, through open democratic processes, determine the types of representation they want and establish objectives and goals that can actually be achieved. One of the notable attributes often cited by anthropologists regarding sustainable Indigenous cultures is their egalitarian nature. Much of what discourages political participation in our current politics is the overwhelming scale and the very real sense that what one thinks does not matter. Apathy and alienation are the byproducts of large-scale, authoritarian organizations, institutions, and governments.

Establishing real local democratic politics leads to greater equality, especially when underrepresented people are given a voice and the means to act. Issues like a livable wage, affordable housing, healthcare, public transportation and healthy air, water, food, and land can be priorities in guiding relocalization efforts. Even large urban areas are comprised of numerous micro communities, all capable of acting autonomously to establish more democratic forms of representation.

The unsustainability of the mega-machine culture of consumer capitalism and authoritarian technics has an expiration date. Cheap energy, climate change, environmental degradation, economic, social, and political inequality are beginning to dismantle the myth of progress and plutocratically organized politics and global economics. It is time to change this trajectory for the sake of humans, nonhumans and the biosphere upon which all life depends before the plutocracy gets any more out of control.

Conclusion

There is simply no way to ignore the ecological overshoot of consumer capitalism and its impacts on the biosphere. Pretending that we can live in a world of endless consumption and growth is infantile and suicidal. The diminishing of biodiversity, the increasing destruction of human and nonhuman life, the economic costs fueled by climate change storms, and the vast inequality created by our current culture is a recipe for apocalyptic scale disaster. No laws or legal apparatus operating within the confines of a culture believing in endless growth and progress construed as technological control over the tyranny of nature is going to resolve our apocalyptic trajectory.

The future, if there is one, lies in a complete transformation of our culture and our relationship with the landbases on which we are rightfully dependent. As Rachel Carson pointed out over half a century ago, human domination and control over nature is an illusion, and it requires through introspection that we turn those ambitions inward, aiming for the mastery of ourselves. Relocalization offers us an alternative vision for thinking about how to utilize our existing physical infrastructure for the purpose of creating autonomous communities grounded in the needs of their landbases. Relocalization contains the potential to democratize our social, political, economic, and environmental interactions and relationships.

References

Anderson, J. E. (1982). "The public utility commission of Texas: A case of capture or rapture?" *Policy Studies Review* 1:484–490.

Barnett, H. C. (1994). *Toxic debts and the superfund dilemma.* Chapel Hill, NC: The University of North Carolina Press.

Bomford, M. (2010). *Getting fossil fuels off the plate.* In R. Heinberg and D. Lerch (Eds.), *The post carbon reader: Managing the 21st century's sustainability crises* (pp. 119–127). Heldsburgh, CA: Watershed Media.

Buhner, S. H. (2006). *Sacred plant medicine: The wisdom in Native American herbalism.* Rochester, NY; Vermont: Bear and Company.

Clifford, M., and T. D. Edwards. (2012). *Environmental crime*, 2nd ed. Burlington, MA: Jones and Bartlett Learning.

Evernden, N. (1999). *The natural alien: Humankind and environment.* Buffalo, NY: University of Toronto Press.

Frank, N. K. and M. Lombness. (1992). *Controlling corporate illegality: The regulatory justice system.* Cincinnati, OH: Anderson Publishing Co.

Glendinning, C. (1994). *My name is Chellis & I'm in recovery from western civilization.* Boston, MA: Shambhala Publications.

Gowdy, J. (1998). *Limited wants, unlimited means: A reader on hunter-gather economics and the environment.* Washington, DC: Island Press.

Jensen, D. (2016). *The myth of human supremacy.* New York, NY: Seven Stories Press.

Kropotkin, P. (2002). *Anarchism: A collection of revolutionary writings.* Mineola, NY: Dover Publications.

Lieberman, D. E. (2013). *The story of the human body: Evolution, health, and disease*. New York, NY: Pantheon Books.

Lynch, M. J., and R. Michalowski. (2006). *Primer in radical criminology: Critical perspectives on crime, power, and identity*. Monsey, NY: Criminal Justice Press.

Manicardi, E. (2012). *Free from civilization: Notes toward a radical critique of Civilization's foundations: Domination, culture, fear, economics, technology*. Salem, MO: Green Anarchy Press.

Mumford, L. (1967). *Technics and human development: The myth of the machine volume one*. New York, NY: Harcourt Brace Jovanovich.

Oelschlaeger, M. (1991). *The idea of wilderness*. New Haven, CT: Yale University Press.

Ponting, C. (1991). *A green history of the world: The environment and the collapse of great civilizations*. New York, NY: Penguin Books.

Seis, M. (2001). Confronting the contradiction: Global capitalism and environmental Health. *International Journal of Comparative Sociology*, XLII (1–2), 123–144.

Shepard, P. (1998). *Nature and madness*. Athens, GA: University of Georgia Press.

Wells, S. (2010). *Pandora's Seed: The unforeseen cost of civilization*. New York, NY: Random House.

Zerzan, J. (1994). *Future primitive and other essays*. Columbia, MO: C.A.L. Press.

Part III
Contemporary Prisoner Voices Within Anarchist Criminology

7. The Staff of Chronos

Reverend David "Wolf Eyes" Rose, Sr.

Why do we as a society kill people to teach others that killing is wrong? The United States of America was founded on some noble principles: Bill of Rights, the U.S. Constitution, etc. Does anyone today even realize where those principles came from? Have we as a society strayed from these principles? My answer would be an emphatic yes!

This chapter is about how the prison system in the U.S. perpetuates itself as an economic entity and how it ignores the true roots of social disorder such as crime and violence. It is about the often, unspoken aspect of the spiritual and moral disintegration of modern culture and society. Finally, I will introduce some ideas about how restorative justice can be used to transform the current state of the prison system and justice system, that will foster education, accountability, healing, responsibility and forgiveness. These ideas are not new, but sometimes they seem to have been forgotten.

Staff of Chronos

I chose the name Staff of Chronos for this paper because of the cyclic nature of time. Also, this title is meant to be a play on words. A "Staff" is linear, which is the way most modern people think. Chronos or Saturn is the God of time in ancient myth, also known as the Grim Reaper or Father of Time. In nature, all time is cyclical. Ancient and indigenous people knew this and applied a cyclical way of thinking to problem solving. Restorative Justice also uses a cyclical way of thinking, which includes a dialogic approach between victim and offender designed to bring about understanding, balance through restitution, relationship, and reconciliation. This idea to use the staff as a symbol of linear thinking, combined with an ancient deity of time (Chronos) came to me while meditating.

What does it mean to you, dear reader, to think about the word "time"? Hours, days, weeks, years? Lifetimes? In prison, you can lose track of time. Your bodily survival takes precedence over everything you may have thought was important in life. Many years ago, I sat in a cell for over three weeks with no property whatsoever. I had only my jeans, a t-shirt, boxers, socks, and a bandana. I had no cup, spoon, toilet paper, not even a bar of soap. There was no T.V., radio, newspaper, magazines, nothing to do but think and feel. The night was long, so long, that my mind had nothing to focus on but fear. I had no hope, no prayers, no one to help me or guide me. I was wrong, however, because I had my mother's unconditional love and that is what brought me back to sanity.

To hear the judge's hammer fall—Blam! "I sentence you to life"! It makes you shudder with tremendous feelings you cannot explain. My mom said, "Life Sentence, what does that even mean"? We had no idea. You have to live it to understand it. Thirty-five years later and I am still living it. Prison is a dark place, and you can lose not only your mind, but your soul and your life. Prison is a huge ware-house of hue-man beings. I say and use the term hue (color)-man because we are all people of color. The government cares nothing about the individuals inside. People chase money, drugs, and material wealth, and kill each other for these things constantly. To survive on a daily basis, you better be ready to defend yourself, because it is just like war. Doing time is your sentence: 10 years, 20 years, 50 years etc. How does one deal with it? You can wallow in fear, get high or drunk all the time, eat, gamble or have sex. You can fight, take from others, kill, seek material comfort at any cost. It is how you live during your time in prison that is what is meant by "doing time." How do you live it? Hard or soft, smart or stupid? Each and every prisoner is like a planet unto himself. It all depends on what kind of prison you are in, as to what is necessary to survive. Malcom X said it best "survive by any means necessary!"

How many wars were actually fought because some sociopath who would, if given the chance, kill anyone who was different from him or herself? What were Korea and Vietnam really about? Why did we send our young men and women over there to struggle, fight, bleed, and die? What is the cost of war? How many people must we sacrifice, not for freedom or justice or individuality, but for economic assets? Wait a minute, what do all these questions have to do with prison, justice and society? It is all connected in a tangled web of factors that reaches into every person's life on planet Earth. Are you surprised that people in a foreign country hate 'Americans', because we drop bombs on innocent civilians, women, children and elders? We call this "Collateral Damage" and make movies about it, because it sells! How impersonal is that? I ask these questions to make you think.

There is not only an interconnectedness between all these subjects but an element that is hardly ever touched upon—spirituality. We train soldiers to Kill, send them into a world of violence, which they acculturate themselves to for personal survival and then bring them back into society and expect them to conform to an authoritative world of order. Are you surprised when they commit an act of violence? What does all this have to do with the subject at hand, you might ask? Everything. The U.S. is a capitalistic society. It is entirely based on "possessing" something that can never be possessed—spiritual fulfillment, land, Mother Earth. An element of hueman existence has been lost, or purposely discarded, by modern society. There is no recognition that all life on Planet Earth is connected in many ways, especially spiritually. Money should not be the most important value of hue-man life.

Indigenous people knew and understood ancient knowledge that modern man has forgotten, overlooked, or discarded because it was inconvenient. Native tribes on "Turtle Island," which the North American continent was called, had no prisons and no written laws. There were, however, moral codes that were kept and remembered, as well as enforced. Prior to colonization, Indigenous peoples did have social problems but nothing comparable to modern society. "Native people carry the same emotional burden as all people of the world. Liars, murderers, rapists, child molesters, thieves and spiritual charlatans lived among First Nation's people. No human being is above any other, all are creations of the Giver of sacred Breath and for that reason all human beings carry the same blessings, burdens, and flaws, in his or her mental, physical and spiritual emotions" (Rev. White Bear Barnard). If someone killed another out of anger or jealously, restorative justice principles were applied by the elders, forgiveness was insisted upon, and personal responsibility for actions was unquestioned. Nonconforming individuals were exiled out of society, never to threaten the welfare of the tribe.

Today's society is seriously out of balance, spiritually, emotionally, mentally, and physically. Nine and ten-year-old children do not need guns or knives. And, they certainly don't need drugs or alcohol to alter their consciousness, regardless of their economic status. You mean to tell me we have the most powerful army in the world and we can't stop drugs and guns from coming into the poorest sections of our cities? When a child is abused, or neglected, he or she is altered by that experience. Often the experience is so psychically traumatic that it is repressed or sublimated. Such horrible things are sometimes too much for an under-developed psyche to process. This goes into the subconscious and remains there, gathering energy until it expresses itself, or is dealt with.

Native and indigenous people had spiritual leaders who were trained to be perceptive on the higher levels of awareness and consciousness. Psychology was understood and practiced, but not written down. These were the inner teachings of the Shamans and Healers that was taught orally and memorized. Ceremonies and rituals were merely tools to help hue-mans deal with emotions of anger, pride, jealousy, etc. Today's society uses powerful forms of media influence (magic really), sight, sound, color, smells, etc., to make money, having no care or concern about how these influences manifest in the hearts and minds of young people.

Prison is an industry. In fact, many prisons are run by private corporations for profit. Prisons employ large workforces, who are basically enslaved whether prisoner or employee, and prisons profit from selling food, toiletries, and clothes to prison populations and employees. The 13th Amendment of the U.S. Constitution abolishes slavery "except as a punishment for crime whereof the party shall have been duly convicted…". Modern day prisons are the legacy of slavery. It costs money to live in a prison. The word penitentiary is derived from the word penitent. Meaning that you sat in your cell and "thought about what you did." This is not what happens in today's prisons. Some are truly barbaric and brutal.

If a native man killed another man of his own tribe, he was asked to apologize to the family of the victim and offer himself in servitude to that family as compensation for their loss. War was more about courage and bravery than the number of dead. Restorative justice meant, if you lost a son who was a hunter and provider by murder, then it was up to the person who committed the offense to fulfill that role. Today no one wants to take responsibility for their own actions. Drug dealers, mobsters, gangsters and killers become themes for popular movies, T.V., and other media. Under developed minds become fascinated by the powerful emotions and adrenaline generated by popular media.

The reality of the U.S. Justice system is often skewed by class, race and power relationships. Why would the justice system hold a person who is innocent, and proven to be innocent of a horrific crime, only because he will not tell the police who actually did it? Why would they let that person die in custody? Punishment is meted out not in accord with justice or compassion, but economically. Sometimes even totally innocent people are sentenced and/or executed because they cannot afford a good attorney, despite U.S. Constitutional protections.

How many of you reading this, could sit in a prison cell, in the dark, no radio, no T.V., no books or magazines, no human contact or conversation whatsoever? Just sit with yourself and your own Mind? It is hard to sit alone in a cell today isolated from everyone that you care about or love. In prison, you are surrounded by hostile people. The darkness and isolation press in on you like a vise, squeezing your mind, body and soul. Everybody wants something from you—whatever they can get. Chronos is time, or rather the ancient deity of "Father Time" or the Grim Reaper, the collector of souls. What would you do if faced with a being that is powerful enough to separate your soul from your body? Let's just assume that this is a real phenomenon and there is a soul, just for the sake of logic in this discussion. Let the Theologians and others argue if it is true or not. That is not the purpose here. Our purpose here is only that of thought and self-reflection.

Each hue-man being has a Biological system that emits both electrical and magnetic signals and fields. These are proven to exist in hue-mans by scientific measurement. Brain waves, nerve impulses, and what Eastern people call "Ki" or "Chi" (energy or what is also called the "breath of life") also exists. Thermal imaging photography can capture Martial Arts Masters demonstrating this phenomenon in motion. Science tells us there are spectrums of light and sound, which the hue-man body cannot see or hear with the ordinary physical senses. It is a fact that people influence other people. Just because some thing is invisible to the hue-man eye, does not mean it does not exist. There are unseen forces such as gravity and many others in the physical world.

Psychology is based entirely on the observation of hue-man behavior. Can you see with your eyes another person's mind? It is my opinion that the human soul has an invisible aspect that can become either balanced or unbalanced. And the key to becoming balanced is the HEART. Compassionate love for another living being and indeed ALL living beings, (i.e., Earth, Trees, Animals) is the key to this balance of the HEART. As Buhner explains:

> The majority of modern peoples, if asked to find the place within their body where the unique self-resides, would say that they live about an inch above their eyebrows and about two inches into the skull. But most indigenous and historical peoples would locate the self some place very different. They would gesture in the region of the heart. For most of our history of habitation on Earth, that is where the seat of intelligence, the seat of the soul, was located. That this has changed is more of an expression of how and what we are taught in Western cultures than of some exact truth. For consciousness is highly mobile and is able to use a variety of locations in the body through which to process the information we receive from the world. (Buhner, 2004, p. 71)

When the hue-man heart becomes closed to love and compassion, it fills with negative emotions such as hate. This is Abnormal Psychology 101, when anger or hate fills the heart a dis-association from reality occurs. This is what occurs in prison from the isolation and disconnection. A person dis-associates from the rest of humanity and believes that she or he is alone and separate from the hue-man race. The hue-man being is the only living being on Earth that can lie to itself, and believe it. A dog will always be a dog, a cat will always be a cat, you get the point. It is only because hue-mans have the ability to reason, that they can convince themselves they are something that they are not.

When Hue-man beings are so dissociated from reality, then and only then, are they capable of becoming able to commit crime and hurt other hue-mans. Because dissociated humans are psychologically and emotionally unbalanced, lacking a moral and ethical framework, they are easily drawn to a criminal mindset. When criminal behaviors are displayed openly in popular culture and media without any type of explanation, undeveloped minds are enamored with a type of power. Killers, gangsters, mobsters, and thieves are presented to young minds in a way that is unrealistic and easily misunderstood. These images influence young impressionable minds and misleads them to "think" its cool to be a criminal.

Negative pop cultural influences combined with the economic inequality that is perpetuated by the ruling class, plus abuse, neglect, lack of guidance, and deprivation of necessities (food, shelter) produces a mindset of, "I'll take what I need." Multiply these conditions by the number of people in the world (7.5 billion), living and suffering in slums and ghettos without the basic necessities of life, along with hate, lust, strife, violence, dissention, war and greed, you get modern society. Many feel it's all just entertainment as long as they can sit safely in their living room and watch it on T.V.

Today's prisons are full of many different kinds of people. The prisons are growing larger by the day as thousands of young people are constantly committing crimes, just to feel a part of something. The gang becomes the family and young minds are desperate for some kind of social acceptance. Most, but not all, have no family or at best, one or two dysfunctional parents also caught up in the modern moral dilemma, commit a crime or go hungry. Then multiply all that by the factor of drug addiction and alcoholism and these kids become an unending stream of cannon fodder for today's prison population.

The answer to all of this is simple, yet complicated. People who are educated and spiritually developed, need to step up and help change the balance of today's moral, ethical and spiritual/psychological imbalances—one soul at a time. That is a lot of work. It will not and cannot happen overnight or in a short period of time. It may take hundreds of years of sustained effort or perhaps even generations.

"Human beings become bestial when they allow themselves to be dominated by their own lower desires and destructive tendencies" (Hall, 2010, p. 153). This is the spiritual aspect of today that is effecting so many young, impressionable minds and influencing them to make very bad choices in their behavior (i.e., crime, violence, greed and lust). Such lower bestial desires are meant to be used as purely physical survival instincts.

Modern culture and society have eliminated the need for hunting and basic survival and instead has preyed upon the base lower desires of hue-man beings in order to make money. This must change and an element of Anarchy is the best method of breaking this pattern. Healing must begin with the individual who has committed a crime. Restorative Justice principles need to be applied on both sides of the coin. Punishment and incarceration does not address the problem, only the symptom (behavior).

Yes, incarceration gets dangerous people off the street by segregation (separation). Yet, incarceration does not change or even address the mental and emotional as well as the spiritual problems in the minds and hearts of young people. Who is paying the millions of dollars to support operational costs of prisons without an emphasis on healing? Rehabilitation is a joke! The majority of people who are paroled are drug addicts, who come right back to prison, perpetuating the prison industrial complex.

Authoritarianism is not the answer. Passing laws, written on paper, will never regulate the hearts and minds of people. Fear of police brutality and intimidation or fear of incarceration or punishment is not the same as respect for human beings and their dignity. People, especially young people, are powerfully influenced by what popular media promotes as the dominant values of today's culture. Until psychologists realize that there is a spiritual component to human beings they will never cure anyone.

When healing happens in an individual it starts with seeing the truth and accepting responsibility for personal actions. Forgiveness is a powerful tool for restoration and balance. Using Restorative Justice principles requires that we, as a race of hue-man beings, educate ourselves in harmony with natural law as well as universal law. This means that those who are rich monetarily must lend their resources back to the rest of the world in order to heal it. Those who are spiritually strong and balanced need to guide those who are lost. This kind of strength and wisdom takes years, perhaps even a life time to acquire. When we begin to mend the minds of people and open their hearts, their compassion, understanding and love will be felt. "Spirituality is having a 'moist Heart', Aboriginal Wisdom knows, the soil of the human Heart is necessarily watered with tears and that tears, keep the ground soft. From soft ground, New Life Is Born" (Chief White Bear Barnard, 2013, p. 19).

For those already incarcerated there must be a way out, a ray of hope. For, if you take away all a person's hope, what type of motivation is there to begin the slow and difficult process of healing through Restorative Justice? This process needs to be chosen by the individual and to be over-seen and controlled by the most ethical and honorable, as well as spiritually developed individuals who have no economic interest in the outcome. It will take time and money to implement the principles of Restorative Justice, so that its effect is meaningful.

The most twisted psychopaths and sociopaths are those souls who have been malformed by abuse and negative influences in their lives. These are the people who need an aspect of spiritual healing most of all. Anyone who has walked through a mental health unit knows the horrors the inmates and patients do to their own bodies just to feel something. Some of these people may never be healed enough to be released in to society, yet they are still worth helping and should be allowed to improve their lives.

There are those of us in prison who have healed ourselves and are no longer a threat to society or anyone else. I can only speak for myself as to my method of healing, and the main elements are love, compassion, and loyalty. If it were not for the love showed to me by my mother, during "my dark night of the soul," I would be lost in my own self, drugged and insane, a mere shell of a soul, sitting in a segregation cell somewhere in this prison system like a sardine in a can. It was acceptance of the past, and helping others through A.V.P. which was the turning point for me. And finally, the spiritual Elders of Pan-American Indian Association Order of Native Practitioners that helped to guide me back to sanity and balance. I had to choose this path. I must also thank the Elders of Sacred Circles Institute and Eagle Voice Center as well as the Human Kindness Foundation, and many others who have guided me to compassion and love.

The main point is that people did not judge me by my past actions and showed me how to find my own spiritual path. This is what we collectively must do for all the people who are either in danger of becoming criminals or are already incarcerated. All are hue-man souls worth saving. What purpose does it serve to keep us locked in cages, if we have changed as human beings? Are you the same person you were thirty-five years ago? We, who have come through the darkness are the best suited and talented to help guide others through the same mental, emotional and spiritual morass. As it is now, there is no end to the suffering and pain we heap upon each other while stacked up in human warehouses like sardines in a can.

Restorative Justice principles must be applied on all levels of the prison system. Diligence, attention to details, and a high degree of spiritual vision must be applied to this task. It will take a massive amount of work and many people working together to accomplish this goal. There is knowledge from the ancient world that can help, as well as from recent brilliant minds such as Carl Jung, Israel Regardie, and Manly P. Hall, just to mention a few.

One very important principle must be applied in order to achieve success. Psychology and understanding of the human mind must include the spiritual aspect. "The difference between Freud's and Jung's approaches to psychology was primarily Jung's view that the human psyche was a whole organism and Freud's belief that it was not" (Regardie, 2002 p. 107). "However, the most notable contribution of Jungian psychology was the concept that individuation was a spiritual excursion and it is highly significant that this pioneer of psychology phrased his ideas in spiritual terms" (Regardie, 2002 p. 109). According to Jung, everyone has a shadow or a dark side and if they are not aware of its existence, then it can overwhelm their lives with darkness and violence. In other words, "if it is repressed and isolated from consciousness, it never gets corrected" (The Collected Works of C.G. Jung, # 11, pg. 131). This is precisely what happens in prison when thousands of unbalanced minds are thrown into a great big mixing bowl and given drugs instead of care and treatment. Medication lines run sometimes, even when the rest of the prison is on "lock down" because of a fight or stabbing.

Restorative Justice means exactly what it says. Justice (not judgement or punishment) must be restored to victims and perpetrators in both secular and spiritual aspects. Hatred and anger toward criminals because of what they did serves no purpose and merely pollutes the spiritual aspect of restorative justice, which breeds more hate and anger.

Forgiveness is one of the most important tools of healing. Criminals must believe there is a real chance that they may earn redemption. If they confront their own faults, make restitution to the victim's family and society, as well as choose to change themselves and heal, they should be allowed to do so. The financial burden on society can be lessened by eliminating prison altogether, yet is this possible without endangering people? This must also be considered. Young minds could be corrected and guided before they are damaged beyond repair by the brutal system of human warehousing and violence, then prisons may become superfluous. Those who are totally irredeemable may still require some form of separation. Everyone, however, should get a chance.

Education is also an essential element of Restorative Justice. Today's primary educational system is not functioning in the best interests of either the children or society. Schools have become a high stress environment where the focus is on fashion and material goods to establish status. Why should young girls think it's not cool to be smart? Students are so overwhelmed by the distractions of consumer culture that it is difficult for them to focus on their intellectual, emotional and spiritual development. Teachers should be viewed as those who guide, sharing knowledge and experience, not demanding memorization of cold facts. We should teach children how to learn, and let them decide what it is that they wish to study, after the basic skills have been successfully grasped. Educators must also realize that each child is a hue-man soul that is undeveloped and requires proper guidance toward discovering her or his true gifts. Each child has unique gifts and abilities to be used to better the individual and the collective culture and society. It is the duty and responsibility of teachers to discern the true gifts and abilities of each child and guide them in the right direction. When these objectives serve as the guiding principles of the educational system, it will become easy to discern which children are not healthy emotionally, and to help them, not ridicule, isolate, or medicate them with powerful drugs. Current methods do not solve the problem and only make it worse. Drugs can be useful; however, they should not be used to make children conform to someone's idea of a correct behavior. Giving children drugs only makes them drug addicts later in life. People must be allowed their individuality. This is also an aspect of the human spirit. Not all hue-man beings are doctors, lawyers, firemen, soldiers and policemen. Hue-man beings do not fit into neat little categories and subcultures. Not everyone is a Medicine Man or a Shaman/Healer. As a race of Hue-man beings we must be perceptive enough to see and allow people to be different. We need a total rebuilding of the educational system. School is where kids learn who they will be when they grow up. If you push them out of school and punish them in prison, prison becomes the school.

Restorative Justice principles need to be applied in the educational setting in order to teach responsibility, self-respect, and honesty in a community setting. Have the reoccurring tragedies in our schools not taught us a lesson about dissociation and alienation? Children don't need guns and we need some form of gun control.

To sum up this chapter, I wish to express two last ideas in the hope that it will make the reader think about the criminal justice in a different light. First of all is a story, analogy or metaphor (whatever you wish to call it) of "Two Wolves." It is a teaching story used by many native elders (and others), in many different forms, all with the same meaning. One day a young child sat down with her/his Grandfather who sat by a fire. The child asked, "Why do people do bad things to each other?" Daughter, Son, the man said, "each hue-man being has two parts or two wolves inside them. One Wolf is good, he is brave, honest, respectful, truthful, loving and compassionate. The other Wolf is bad or evil, he is hateful, angry, lustful, greedy, and self-centered, violent, and unbalanced. These two Wolves struggle to control the person's mind." "But Grandpa," the child said, "which one wins?" "Which one do you feed?" Grandpa answered. This is the struggle within all hue-man beings. Each of us has a higher nature and a lower nature.

The second point is that we as Hue-man beings must realize that we are all connected, related, and living on the same planet. We all breathe the same air. We all walk upon the same planet. Our souls and bodies are made of common elements. The Earth is our Mother, giving birth to the physical forms of our bodies. We will all leave our bodies here on Earth and move on. What do you believe? We natives have a saying, in a thousand different languages, that all mean the same thing. Mitakuye Oyasin (Mee-tah-koo-yay O-yah-seen), Gus'di Os'dah dah duhni (Goo-See dee O-see-da-da-duh-knee)—WE ARE ALL RELATED! WE ARE ALL CONNECTED!

References

Buhner, H. (2004). *The secret teachings of plants: the intelligence of the heart in the direct perception of nature.* Rochester, VT: Bear & Co.

Chief White Bear Barnard. (2013). *Teaching fellowship. Pan American Indian Association.* p. 19.

Hall, M. P. (1928/2010). *The secret teachings of all ages.* Mineola, NY: Dover Publications.

Regardie, I. (2002). *The middle pillar: the balance between mind and magic*, 3rd ed. C. Cicero & S. T. Cicero (Eds.). Woodbury, MN: Llewellyn Publications.

Rose, D. E. (2011). *A view from a shelf.* Unpublished.

8. *Actual Connections to Slavery in the Prison System*

MAURICE L. GRAHAM

Introduction

Knowing that prison is a continuation of slavery is important in the fight for transformative justice and abolition. If we buy into the mythos that the penal system is a natural manifestation of democratic societies' efforts to provide public safety, then we fall behind the curve of history, losing sight of the roots of our current police state along with our ability to do something productive about our situation. Consequently, it is important that in addition to our passionate feelings about what is just, right, and progressive, we have some reasonably articulable factual basis available to inform our ethics.

College students and activists are talking about the federal government's connections to the cocaine and heroin trade, and the focus thereon has largely been one that revolves around reduction of drug criminalization and/or reductions in minority/white sentencing disparities. What is posited here, however, is that government manipulation of justice policy runs deeper than simply an excursion into the drug trade. This section excerpts a larger unpublished work of mine entitled "A Report on the Psychodynamics of the Penal System" that explores connections between the Peculiar Institution's struggles for survival and the gradual birth of incarceration nation and mass felonization. While it is impactful to hear, as I have heard, the personal testimonies of elderly Hmong about CIA bases that extract and transport heroin, we must understand that this is merely a symptom of a criminal justice system birthed into corruption and whose purpose is to perpetuate the same. What it comes down to is this: the prison system has little to do with public safety, and everything to do with preserving slavery as a profit-making mechanism in the face of popular discontent; anything short of abolition provides a lifeline to every enemy of progress in our midst, and until we recognize this and develop alternative methods to replace it the rest of our systems will continue to fail—right along with our happiness, our freedom, and our pocketbooks.

Modern Roots of Dysfunction

The ideas of states' rights, slavery, and fascism were strong enough to rally a nation to war, and they were strong enough to survive defeat. We saw this with the emergence of Jim Crow, and we must not be so foolish as to think the economic imperative dissipated merely because the will of the people carried the day.

In 1871, immediately after the Civil War, Virginia courts were conspicuously quick to point out that although the 13th Amendment abolished slavery, that provision didn't apply to convicted felons. "The Bill of rights, though made part of the present constitution, has the same force and authority, and no more, than it always had. And the principles which it declares have reference to freemen, and not to convicted felons" (Ruffin, 1871). Richmond, Virginia was the capital of the Confederate States of America, and less than six years after Lincoln was assassinated, their courts were pointing out the loopholes in constitutional law. This is not the expression of a contrite and repentant prodigal; it is the sentiment of an ardent foe. The slave states were determined to prevail, to snatch the Union victory before things had time to settle, and were quick to stake their claim. The confederates had lost black chattel slaves, but they wanted felons in return.

Apparently the confederates realized that what they couldn't win on the battlefield could be recouped in friendly courtrooms. The Union may have rallied forces to uphold the integrity of the nation, but no such resources could be mustered on behalf of those who were clearly in disfavor, i.e., convicted felons. The Supreme Court of Virginia—which we shouldn't forget was the capital state of the confederacy—did not leave any doubts as to its intention to lawfully sanction the enslavement of convicts. "For the time being, during his term of service in the penitentiary, he is in a state of penal servitude to the state … He is for the time being the slave of the state" (Ruffin, 1871). That's very strong language, especially considering the context at the time.

After such rulings, the ex-confederate states proliferated laws that history calls Black Codes. These laws had one aim: to define and limit the rights of former slaves after the Civil War. Clearly the South was not ignorant to the fact that their Trojan Horse was the criminal justice system. Despite pledges of fealty to the prevailing Union, and overtures of reconciliation, the South was replete with nostalgia for their former condition. This is critical because, as the United States Commission on Civil Rights noted: "The jury is perhaps the most important instrument of justice. For jury service is the only avenue of direct participation in the administration of justice open to the ordinary citizen" (1961). With the ordinary citizens of the South predisposed to aiding in the re-enslavement of Blacks, the southern criminal justice system was uniquely situated to lay the groundwork for a gigantic, legal, plantation system.

The uprising throughout the South after ratification of the 15th Amendment in 1870 is ample testament to this sentiment. Of particular importance to abolitionists, it was found that, "By 1872, the legislative and executive branches of state government ... were once again firmly in the control of white Democrats, who resorted to a variety of tactics, including fraud, intimidation, and violence, to take away the vote from Blacks..." (Mcdonald, 2003, n.p.)

In recap, we have the 15th Amendment in 1870, five years after Lincoln's assassination; the Ruffin v Commonwealth ruling by the Virginia Supreme Court delegating felons as slaves in 1871; and by 1872 we find that through intimidation, fraud, and brutality the government throughout the South was again in the hands of confederates. 1870, 1871, 1872 ... this is an organized, concerted effort to preserve slavery by any means. The Civil War did not end the South; it forced them to turn toward more vulnerable prey, i.e., felons, as a path toward regaining their former strength. As the Black Codes settled in, and astute abolitionists and blacks fought the Apartheid style policies of the Jim Crow era, the confederacy perfected its transition.

In the sixties, a new Voting Rights Act abolished everything that even looked like racial suppression. This is because, as is stated in the 2007 Public Policy Manual, "In 1965, it was perfectly reasonable to believe that any move affecting black enfranchisement in the Deep South was deeply suspect." (Thernstrom). Unfortunately, the move being made in the South was toward controlling the criminal justice system, and this was less transparent to the progressive masses. Thus, when the Confederacy found itself cornered by progressive policies they had the foresight to heap propaganda onto the populace at large, frightening everyone into enacting criminal laws to control the now free—and supposedly feral—Blacks. Subsequently, cautious steps were taken toward civil rights, while new laws and new penitentiaries were created as a safeguard. But this new phase was no safeguard at all; it was a calculated step toward facilitating the felonization of the populace and thereby maintaining slavery.

Felonies have long disenfranchised, but never in the history of American democracy had so many things become felonies nor prosecutions become so absolute and devoid of oversight by the affected public until the Confederacy's takeover of the criminal justice system in America. An articulate and literate U.S. Supreme Court recognized the Trojan Horse and attempted to close the breech by declaring prisoners retain whatever constitutional rights they had in freedom, so long as they didn't interfere with the safety and secure operation of the prisons.

Although welcome, the rulings in Mcdonnell were not enough to stem the tide unleashed by our modern Trojan Horse. Chief Justice Berger noted: "To sanction disrespect and disregard for the Constitution in the name of protecting society from lawbreakers is to make the Government itself lawless and to subvert those values upon which our ultimate freedom and liberty depend" (Stone v Powell, 1976). The Confederacy undermined the criminal justice system. As demonstrated in the historic cases that cover over a century since the official Civil War until the Voting Rights Act in the 1960s, the Confederate threat adapted and found new ways to thrive. They used the criminal justice system to thwart the Black vote and re-enslave the masses—and this assault continues.

Continuing Dysfunction

In Hunter (1985), it was revealed that the assaults on the Black vote continued to be successful up to that ruling. The assault was said to have originated in the official proceedings of the Constitutional Convention of the state of Alabama, and others throughout the South, to, in the delegates' words, "Within the limits imposed by the Federal Constitution, to establish white supremacy" (1985, n.p.). That case was over 10 years after Mcdonald.

Like the courts have noted, the jury is the most important instrument of justice. Logic would dictate, then, that the determination of the effectiveness of our criminal justice system hinges upon evaluating the effectiveness of our juries. Into the l980s, discrimination in jury selection was rampant, prompting Justice Thurgood Marshall to predict that court rulings intended to stop the unconstitutional use of race in jury selection would be ineffective unless we "eliminate peremptory challenges entirely" (Batson v Kentucky, 1986). That illustrates how critically pervasive the use of racialized juries to oppress citizens was at the time.

In 2003 it was found that little had changed. That year a court outlined how, "the state had peremptorily challenged 12% of qualified nonblack panel members, but eliminated 91% of the black ones." That court further stated, "The state's pretextual positions confirm Miller's claim, and the prosecutor's own notes proclaim that the Sparling Manual's emphasis on race was on their minds when they considered every potential juror." The court finally recognized the need to correct injustice; however, the court's ruling came, as itself acknowledged, after "17 years of largely unsuccessful and protracted litigation—including 8 different judicial proceedings, and 8 different judicial opinions, and involving 23 judges" (Miller-El v Dretke, 2005). This is spectacular evidence that pro-slavery reasoning in the judiciary remains steadfast.

Confederate-spawned initiatives to felonize Americans have not been confirmed to the South. The criminal justice system truly was a magnificent Trojan Horse. Even online, SmartJury Product Information blatantly delivers prosecutors handy data for circumventing the Constitution's prohibition against depriving Blacks and other citizens of the right to sit on juries. In the work The Use of Peremptory Challenges in Capital Murder Trials, Philadelphia, in a study of 317 capital cases from 1981 to 1997, it was found to be engaged in the same process as the court identified in the Miller-El case (Baldus et al., 2001). This was not exceptional. In case study after case study, from DC, Texas, Colorado, Minnesota, California, and elsewhere, the Confederacy—through its proxy corrections business machine, has corrupted the American criminal justice system in a manner that renders it both untenable, and unconscionable.

Understanding the Truth About Injustice

In 1870 the l5th Amendment passed, strengthening voting rights of former slaves, and hindering their return to servitude. In 1871 the South revealed felonization as the ultimate Trojan Horse. In 1888, the 50th congress, 1st session, 14, reprints an article from the Jackson Daily Mississippian saying, "We further warn any and all negroes of this city against attempting, at their utmost hazard, by vote or influence, to foist on us again this black and damnable machine miscalled a government." In 1898, a victorious mayoral candidate in Wilmington, North Carolina urged whites to, "Go to the polls tomorrow, and if you find a negro out voting, tell him to leave the polls, and if he refuses kill him; shoot him down in his tracks" (Tolnay and Beck, 1995, 67). Though the South's violent antics risked reprisal by the Union forces in this post-reconstruction era, they openly explored all options to maintain the vestiges of the Confederacy. Like was said at the Alabama Constitutional Convention of 1901, "And what is it that we want to do? Why it is within the limits imposed by the Federal Constitution, to establish white supremacy" (Knox, 1901, 8).

Through proclamations like these, the Confederacy announced its transition from relying only upon open violence and unconstitutional intimidation, to legitimizing their treasonous activities through legislative actions now known as the Black Codes. As the progressives awoke to the Confederacy's belligerence—and Blacks resisted—violent oppression occurred, giving a glimpse to the perspicacity of the South's wresting of complete control over the organs of criminal justice in that region.

A 1965 New York Times article reported: "It is now clear that the public officials and the police of Alabama are at war with those citizens who are Negroes and who are determined to exercise their rights under the constitution of the United States" (Banner, 1965, E11). As the United States Supreme Court identified, there is an "Insidious and pervasive evil which had been perpetuated in certain parts of our country through unremitting and ingenious defiance of the Constitution." (Katzenbach, 1966).

The greater tragedy is that the system hasn't been inclined to adopt the activist position necessary to correct itself. In 1998, the federal courts ruled, "State prisoner's 1983 15th Amendment challenge to state constitutional provisions disenfranchising him as convicted felon must fail ... because mere fact that many incarcerated felons happen to be black and Latino is insufficient grounds to implicate 15th Amendment." (Jones v Edgar, 1998). True to the Confederate formula, such a ruling sounds reasonable when completely divorced and insulated from the sharp realities of the courts, and the courts' own experience. Within context, however, it would be foolish to ignore the implications for our citizenry.

To paraphrase Republican Steve Atwater, on Reagan's "Southern Strategy" in the 1980s, "It's no longer acceptable to run around saying "Nigger, Nigger, Nigger" you must couch your feelings in acceptable ways such as states' rights, or a parent's rights to choose their children's schools." Likewise, in the present, it's not acceptable to speak directly of the slave populace, this discussion must be sanitized by the terms, convicted felon, predatory offender, or criminal. Once the subject is thoroughly disinfected such misleading and prejudicial terminology, then disenfranchisement becomes not only feasible, it becomes reasonable.

The purpose of disenfranchisement is slavery. This protects profit, hence, the emphasis upon the status of both prisoners and slaves as property. This correlates to several million felons in our country being identified not by name but by correctional department number, exactly as merchandise is treated in a business. The proliferation of new categories of crimes and felonies is facilitated by the fact that slavery is profitable, at least, for the particular type of businessman it attracts.

With over 2 million people incarcerated in jails and prisons, the United States is the world leader in imprisonment, both in the absolute numbers of prisoners and in incarceration rate. China, with one billion more people than the United States, has 1.5 million fewer prisoners. We spend over $200 billion each year to fund the criminal justice system, while the total economic loss from crime a year around is $15.6 Billion. The average costs per crime for each victim stood at $100, yet the average cost spent incarcerating each criminal crime stood at $64,000 (Austin et al., 2007).

This is an absolutely and completely unfathomable circumstance; completely unfathomable that is, unless you know the history. Slavery, from a historical perspective, has been a profitable endeavor, and susceptibility to enslavement is attribute to disenfranchisement—which prevents afflicted communities from effectively rallying against the detrimental policies and tactics of this chattel-commerce business.

The Foundational Logic and Formative Influences of Prison Policy

In 1870, the first meeting by the National Prison Association, the precursor to the American Correctional Association, was held in Cincinnati (Keve, 1991). The goal was to establish principles to guide corrections in the United States and Europe. Even though these principles were expanded in 1982, the basic ideals haven't undergone any major changes since their inception.

It is significant that the first president of the National Prison Association was Rutherford B. Hayes and that, although he was inactive during his presidency of the U.S., he resumed leadership of the organization after his executive term ended. The significance of President Hayes's role lay in the fact that he was the President who got the Republican Party to end Reconstruction and withdraw federal troops from the South. Without federal oversight, the federal courts lost influence in secessionist states and the southern judiciary immediately reverted to Confederate control.

To explain more clearly, Rutherford B. Hayes was awarded the presidency of the United States by the electoral commission in 1876. In order to get the South to acquiesce to the commission's ruling, the Compromise of 1877 was enacted, whereby the Republican Party agreed to withdraw U.S. troops in exchange for Southern support for the election of Rutherford B. Hayes (Orth, 1987). The most overt effect was that the Confederate states rapidly began repudiating the debt they'd accrued during the Civil War via friendly courts. With all of the attention this acquired Confederate consolidation of the criminal justice system went relatively unnoticed (Gibbons, 1981).

The clear implication is that Rutherford B. Hayes was the original president of the National Prison Association expressly to facilitate Confederate control over American prisoners as a replacement for the loss of chattel slavery. Several situations color this viewpoint. First, if the timelines of the Southern takeover of the criminal justice system are examined it will be noticed that during the entire period of its inception Rutherford B. Hayes was either President of the United States or President of the National Prison Association. Further shedding light is the fact that Mr. Hayes headed the NPA until his death in 1893, indicating his commitment to bolstering the fledgling institution.

Second, President Hayes's replacement, Roeliff Brinkerhoff, pushed for nonpartisan administration of prisons. This relatively innocuous fact would seem unremarkable, even laudable, if the timelines are ignored. At that period in American history there were only two parties, those for salvaging the Confederacy, and those for strengthening the Union. In effect, then, nonpartisan meant delivering pro-slavery politicians an equal say in creating the American system of criminal justice.

Finally, the election of President Hayes was contingent upon the withdrawal of federal troops from Confederate territories and reversion to Southern control of the judiciary. As a criminal lawyer the significance of this compromise wouldn't have been lost on him and lends strong credence to the view of his complicity in the Confederate takeover of the criminal justice system.

Whether President Hayes was actually a conspirator with the Confederacy or was simply forced by political circumstances to strengthen their position in the criminal justice system is relevant to his legacy but has no effect upon the aftermath of his decisions. Prison was plainly placed into the hands of pro-slavery elements.

By all appearances the declarations arising out of the first meeting of the National Prison Association were progressive for their time and this appears due to the influence of President Hayes. He emphasized that crime was an effect and not a cause, and this was reflected in the NPA's position that "moral regeneration" was possible. Under the racialized culture of the times, however, it was generally understood that no one was more degenerate than former slaves and their associates. Moreover "moral regeneration" had always been a part of the equation justifying slavery, and an important role of the antebellum master was the rescue of the inferior races from their natural degeneracy through bondage to whites.

If this seems incredulous, then the following passage from Dred Scott is enlightening:

> That neither the class of persons who had been imported as slaves, nor their descendants, whether they had become free or not, were then acknowledged as a part of the people, nor intended to be included in the general words used in that instrument [the Constitution] ... they [persons with African blood] had for more than a century before been regarded as beings of an inferior race, and altogether

> unfit to associate with the white race, either in social or political relations, and so far inferior that they had no rights which the white man was bound to respect, and that the negro might justly and lawfully be reduced to slavery for his benefit; [Emphasis mine]. (Dred Scott v Sandford, 1856)

NPA's lofty language notwithstanding, the South was heavily invested at this critical time period in preserving slavery through the language of the law and this thoroughly colored the wording of the law as applied to criminals. In fact, it may be argued that the entire logic of prison itself transformed to accommodate its usage as a surrogate plantation system. To find credence for this argument one need look no further than the congressional discussions surrounding the Civil Rights Act of 1866.

The full scope of the arguments surrounding Reconstruction are beyond the scope of this inquiry, however, when speaking of the roots of modern prison logic that era is the indisputable forerunner of our conversation. For instance, Angola prison in Louisiana was established in 1834 and its primary purpose was to profit off of the convict-lease system. Although this love affair with profiteering off of crime was briefly severed during the Civil War, this business arrangement resumed full force in 1868—exactly the time period this notebook questions. This reinstatement was specifically tailored to make up for the labor shortage resulting from the abolishment of slavery, and, importantly, the vast majority of its 222 prisoners were Black and under 25 years of age (Carleton, 1971).

None of this states that slavery was the only factor in the development of prison logic, just that it was the major driver in the development of policy which still affects us today. That the other prison models, such as the Eastern and Auburn systems, bowed completely to the Southern agenda is, however, apparent.

In the first place, the Auburn system already had labor at the center of its rehabilitative planning. The inaugural prison factory was launched as early as 1824, and this made permanent the place of inmate labor. Naturally, this role of prison as a labor supplement was complimentary to Confederate designs and the Auburn system spread as a way to rebuild the South after the Civil War (Cullen & Travis III, 1984).

Secondly, the English system which predated the American system openly was predicated upon utilizing felons as slaves. A common punishment in colonial England was sentencing to being transported, or being shipped to labor as an indentured servant in one of the English colonies; the fact that slave masters in the South used this scheme heavily as a way to discipline unruly slaves demonstrates a clear continuity of policy (Gildemeister, 1987).

Finally, though we often pay attention to the idealism of early prison reformers, prison itself actually was completely understood as enslavement. Thus, whenever we talk about the foundations of prison philosophy our conversation takes on the tone of a Confederate apologist. We must rationalize and explain away the racist and degenerate substance of the system itself in an effort to extoll its corollary virtues. However we wile it away, prisoners would likely still openly be chattel slaves if not for the activism of workers' unions. Even with this accidental ally, changes to the prison system were more form than substance.

American labor, through such means like the Hawes-Cooper Act in 1929 and the Ashurst-Sumners Act in 1935, cut short the competition from prison slave labor, however, these pro-labor provisions did nothing to change the actual policy that the rules of criminal justice were premised upon. As was noted earlier in this document, no changes were made to the basic ideals of criminal justice until 1982, and those were not structural.

One difficulty in understanding the logic of prison—and felonization in general—is the lack of historical perspective. Briefly, prisoners were openly considered slaves of the state during the formative period of prison policy. When the tide of the rest of the country turned toward Reconstruction and the amalgamation of America's new citizens of color, prisons predominantly remained under local control. By the time any efforts at reform were advanced federalist principles protected long-entrenched, racially and pro-slavery motivated policy, something the courts have never been able to undo.

Federalism dictated that certain activities of state government shouldn't be micromanaged by the federal government, and in the aftermath of the Civil War states energetically protected what sovereignty remained to them (Alexander, 1994). This resulted in the racialized and pro-slavery components of prison remaining relatively untouched by the other changes sweeping the nation. With this set of circumstances the premise of modem prison logic and policy emerged.

The Process of Preserving Slavery Through Criminal Justice

Authorized histories of corrections in the United States candidly relay the early existence of barbaric and inhumane practices within this nation's prisons. Their goal is to explain and document the roots of current practices in the light of changing and often progressive philosophies. The quest to be empirical is sound practice, but it ignores the one facet of the system that isn't adequately documented: corruption.

Penologists are quick to cite corruption as the cause of major philosophical failures in the history of American criminal justice. It is blamed for unduly harsh treatment, irresponsible leniency, convict exploitation by private industry, convict exploitation by other prisoners, riots, exorbitant profits, unfair competition with the free market, financial insolvency, and failed public safety. Politicians at all levels have sought to correct these deficiencies through a variety of legislation addressing each of these circumstances individually. What the nation has collectively failed to do, however, is address the slippery slope premise that public safety lay in either capital punishment or incapacitation.

The degrading of human rights is the only path to slavery. By whatever justification, felonization does in fact degrade human rights. It limits your voting rights and rights to housing, working, and relocating free from discrimination. It stigmatizes and sanctions discrimination in the public and private arena. It lowers the quality of citizenship. Felonization, then, is an antithesis to liberty and therefore a corrupting influence upon our democratic society.

To understand the connections, a short questioning of the language of slavery and the language of criminal justice and prisons is necessary. For example, prisons have an internal court system that operates differently from the standard courts of America. Their concern is only with meting out punishment, as in their opinion due process is a security threat. Even if prisoners are not guilty of alleged institutional infractions, prison officials discipline them anyhow because they cannot permit the inference that the reporting guard can be wrong (Kassebaum, Ward, and Wilner, 1971).

This is actually an unsafe practice for the order of the institution as well as the safety of the public whom will receive large numbers of ex-convicts returning to the community thoroughly schooled in injustice and callous indifference. It is clearly a policy that has its roots in the perverse style of white nationalism prevalent in antebellum America where the master was always right and the slaves, people of color, and women could be disregarded.

Other notable connections between prison policy and slave codes can be identified in the conducting of strip and body cavity searches, before and after visitation with family, even if the visit is non-contact; the compelling of inmates to address the guards with polite terminology without receiving the same consideration in return; scorn for philosophical reflection and advanced book learning; immediate obedience to guards regardless of the quality of the request; disruptive and arbitrary punishments for ill-defined infractions such as disrespect toward staff, reckless eyeballing, insolence, verbal jousting, dividing staff, improper display of identification, movement pass not visible, and disallowance of cellmates to exit the cell while the other occupant defecates, including the policy of prohibiting the door to remain open while the cell ventilates after such bowel movements (The American Bar Association, 1974).

None of the aforementioned common practices within prison carry any semblance of a relation to the actual safety of the public or the prison. Yet it is difficult to convey to the lay person the extra connections between these petty policies and the system of slavery which dogs and holds back our society. Moreover, law-abiding citizens aren't readily able to draw connections between these practices and the deteriorating status of their livelihoods. To provide a hand, a little review is necessary.

Alexis de Tocqueville and Gustav de Beaumont, while touring the U.S. prison system for the government of France in 1833 stated, "In those states in which there exist one Negro to thirty whites the prisons contain one Negro to four white persons" (61–62). The states referred to by them were northern and border states and so it is easy to see that the South's philosophy affected the North's administration of justice toward people of color and other undesirables.

After the Civil War, chain gangs in many states originally only contained Blacks, and this continued until the 1970s. Prisons were used as a way to manage ex-slaves, and by 1870 90% of convicted felons in the South were Blacks. From 20% to 40% died in a given year, and this was from beatings and the like which continued unabated from slavery, often with slave overseers serving as prison Wardens or convict labor overseers.

The food on chain gangs mimicked slave fare, consisting of a square of corn pone, three slices of fried pig fat, and a dose of sorghum. On holidays there were only 2 meals instead of 3 (still a current practice even in northern prisons such as Minnesota), and indigent hygiene care was practically nonexistent (Ayres, 1984).

After emancipation, Blacks were funneled into penal institutions in what many at the time saw explicitly as a recasting of slavery. A Mississippi Grand Jury investigating conditions of convicts reported that, "Most of them have their backs cut in great wales, scars, and blisters, some with skin peeling off in pieces as the result of severe beatings … they are lying there dying, some of them on bare boards, so poor and emaciated that their bones almost come through their skin, many complaining for want of food … we actually saw live vermin crawling over their faces…" (Sellin, 1976, 148).

During the so-called birth years of the modern and enlightened prison philosophies, Enoch Wines and Theodore Dwight both reported that the rehabilitation of prisoners in 1867 was a fallacy and that, "One string is harped upon, ad nauseam—money, money, money." Prison clearly has always been about slavery and its profits, and this element has not changed (Wines & Dwight, 1867, 289).

Originally, prison industry paid prevailing wages to prisoners with deductions for cost of tools and board, scaled to skills; this was organized under a public account system. Overcrowding in the early 1800s led to the demise of this system. Convicts unable to pay a fee were sold into slavery and sent to work by their owner. Gallery slavery allowed 20% of prevailing wages in the

17th and 18th centuries to go to the slave. Coincidentally (or not), current Prison Industry Enhancement pay scale mandates a 20% split to prisoner and 80% to the needs of the state or private operator of the prison industry (Bettag, 1957; DOJ, 1999).

Confronting Bias

That prison logic is the logic of slavery is irrefutable and presents a fundamental question to all of us who believe in liberty: is slavery, for whatever reason, an acceptable part of our American reality? At this juncture, it is appropriate to look at some of the thinking that any conversation about felonization or criminal justice evolution inherently reverts to. It was said in Bell, "It is better for all the world, if instead of waiting to execute degenerate offspring for crime, or to let them starve for their imbecility, society can prevent those who are manifestly unfit from continuing their kind..." (Buck v Bell, 1927). That is harsh speaking indeed, but typical considering the prevailing attitudes at the time.

The prejudicial and controversial thinking style concerning society's niggers, i.e. lower classes, extends back as far as can be researched and indeed is a founding principal of the thinking that has went into our current treatment of felons. In the 1700s Blackstone wrote, "[T]he keeping one day in the seven holy, as a time of relaxation and refreshment as well as for public worship, is of admirable service to a state considered merely as a civil institution. It humanizes, by the help of conversation and society, the manners of the lower classes; which would otherwise degenerate into a sordid ferocity and savage selfishness of spirit; it enables the industrious workman to pursue his occupation in the ensuing week with health and cheerfulness." (BL. Commentary. 63)

An English statute in 1788 set controls over the religious activities of the poor, and outlined their hours of work (28 Georgetown III, c. 48). Rhode Island's 1679 preamble provided that Sunday employment was banned because "persons being evil minded, have presumed to employ in servile labor, more than necessity requireth, their servants...." (3 Records of the Colony, 31). This type of thinking wasn't merely hypothetical; it resulted in the horrors of the experiments upon prisoners lasting up until the 1970s where malaria, syphilis, cancer, and genital irradiation were utilized upon the incarcerated populace as a precursor to the sale of drugs upon the free market (Healy, 1994; Morris, 1974).

Much of what outwardly ailed the prison-slavery system was ameliorated by the rise of the medical model in the 1950s, culminating in prison programs based upon vocational training, group therapy, education, and case-based treatment programming. Along with quasi-progressive court rulings such as Wolff v. Mcdonnell this has contributed to the perception that the criminal justice system separated itself from slavery. Underlying these reforms, however, still lay the slave codes which are the foundation of prison policy in this century. Until the last vestiges of the Peculiar Institution are eliminated from positions of power in our social discourse the welfare of our citizens will continue to deteriorate.

Political strife is something that has become epidemic, especially with the increasing visibility of immigrants, minorities, and women in positions of great power. White Citizens Councils, the creators and sponsors of the Ku Klux Klan, became what are now called Conservative Citizens Councils. Old Confederate ideology has given credence to this branch of society which couches blatant racism and sexism in politically correct terminology—which, curiously is only the Rebel South verbiage minus the name-calling—that speaks of states' rights and separatism as an exercise in moral selectivity for the protection of their children against the evil halls of government. This conveniently forgets that the South never considered the government an instrument of evil until Reconstruction, and such vitriolic attacks are a continuation, unbroken, of that civil conflict.

The vibrancy and life with which Antebellum Southern thinking disrupts our body politic is the direct result of its never having been deprived of its stronghold: slavery. As long as slavery exists, arguments placing a humane face upon exploitation will continue to advance themselves, taking on a life of their own and justifying the perpetuation of ill in our midst. We need to heed the words of Frederick Douglass and pay attention to the new skin this snake of our past has emerged with, and once and for all, stamp our foot down firmly upon the side of justice and liberty for everyone.

Conclusion

The overall objective is that an alternative to incarceration be grafted into our criminal justice system in place of the current prison-industrial complex. Nowhere does the constitution indicate a preference for how a convicted citizen is brought to justice—merely that justice does in fact occur.

An alternative to incarceration—most likely a system trifurcated to separately work with mental health, substance addiction, and social issues—could be an opportunity to develop a law enforcement agent that worked in tandem, instead of in contention with, the constitution. If a system dedicated to prevention and transformative justice by chance results in some escaping complete retribution, then that is not more offensive to our dignity or our constitution than its opposite occurring. In a 1928 case, Justice Holmes said it is "a less evil that some criminals should escape than that the Government should play an ignoble part." With equitable changes, wrought of compassion, vision, and love of liberty, our justice system can yet reclaim the torchlight that brightens our path toward a more perfect union.

References

3 Records of Rhode Island and Providence Plantations 31. (1679). Preamble of Rhode Island. Rhode Island Colony.

Alexander, R. (1994). Hands off, hands semi-off: A discussion of the current legal test used by the United States Supreme Court to decide inmates' rights. *Journal of Crime and Justice*. 17(1): 103–128.

Austin, J., Clear, T., Duster, T., Greenberg, D. F., Irwin, J., McCoy, C., Mobley, A., Owen, B., & Page, J. (2007). *Unlocking America: Why and how to reduce America's prison population*. Washington, DC: JFA Institute.

Ayres, E. (1984). *Vengeance and justice: Crime and punishment in the 19th century American south*. New York: Oxford University Press.

Baldus, D.C., Woodworth, G., Zuckerman, D., & Weiner, N. A. (2001). *The use of peremptory challenges in capital murder trials: A legal and empirical analysis, 3U. Pa. J. Const. L. 3.* http://scholarship.law.upenn.edu/jcl/vol3/iss1/2

Banner, W. A. (1965). Aid for Selma Negroes. *New York Times*. March 14. E11.

Bettag, O. (1957). Use of prison inmates in medical research. *American Journal of Corrections*. 19(3): 4–29.

BL Commentary. (n.d.). 4 Bl. Comm. 63.

Carleton, M. (1971). *Politics and punishment: The history of the Louisiana state penal system*. Baton Rouge: Louisiana State University Press.

Cook, M. (1866). *39th Congress, 1st Session*. Congressional globe, p. 1123.

Cullen, F., & Travis III, L. (1984). New England Journal on Civil and Criminal Confinement.

De Beaumont, G., & de Tocqueville, A. 1833. *On the penitentiary system in the United States and its application in France*. Philadelphia, PA: Carey, Lea, and Blanchard.

Department of Justice. 1999. PIECP Final Guidelines.

Georgetown. (n.d.). 28 Geo. III, c. 48.

Gibbons. (1981). "83 Columbia Law Review at 1981." *Columbia Law Review*.

Gildemeister, G. A. (1987). *Prison labor and convict competition with free workers in industrializing America, 1840–1890*. New York: Garland.

Healy, M. (1994). Science of power and weakness. *Los Angeles Times*. January 8. pp. Section A, 1, 12.

Kassebaum, G., Ward, D., & Wilner, D. (1971). *Prison treatment and parole survival: An empirical assessment*. New York: Wiley.

Keve, P. (1991). Prisons and the American conscience.

Knox, J. B. (May 21st, 1901, to September 3rd 1901). "Opening address." Official proceedings of the constitutional convention of the state of Alabama, (p. p. 8).

Mcdonald, L. (2003). *A voting rights odyssey: Black enfranchisement in Georgia*.

Morris, N. (1974). *The future of imprisonment.* Chicago: University of Chicago Press.
(n.d.). Retrieved 2007, from http://www.cts-america.com/smartjury pi.asp.
Notices. (April 17, 1999). PIECP program federal register. *American Journal of Corrections.* 64(66).
Orth, J. (1987). *Judicial power of the United States: The Eleventh Amendment in American History* 53–57.
Sellin, J. T. (1976). *Slavery and the penal system.* New York: Elsevier.
The American Bar Association. (1974). *Survey of prison disciplinary practices and procedures.*
The Vera Institute. (2013). Retrieved April 2014, from The Vera Institute.
Thernstrom. (n.d.). Section 5 of the Voting Rights Act: By Now, A Murky Mess, 5 600 JL.
Tolnay, S. E., & Beck, E. M. (1995). A festival of violence: An analysis of southern lynchings, 1882–1930. Urbana-Champaign, IL: University of Illinois Press.
United States Commission on Civil Rights. 1961. Justice. 89.
Wines, E. C., & Dwight, T. W. (1867). *Report on the prisons and reformatories of the United States and Canada.* Albany, NY: van Benthutsen.

Cases Cited

Batson v. Kentucky, 476 US 79, 106 S.Ct 1712, 90 L.Ed 2d 69 (The Supreme Court 1986).
Buck v. Bell, 274 US 200, 71 Ed 1000, 47 S.Ct. 584 (The Supreme Court 1927).
Dred Scott v. Sandford, 15 LED 691, 19 How 393 (The Supreme Court May 12, 1856).
Hunter v. Underwood and Edwards etc., 471 US 222, 85 L.Ed 2d 222, 105 S.Ct 1916 (The Supreme Court April 16, 1985).
Jones v. Edgar, 510 US 1027, 126 L.Ed 2d 601, 1993 US LEXIS 7894 (The Supreme Court December 13, 1993).
Miller-El v. Doug Dretke, Director,Texas Department of Criminal Justice, Correctional Institutions Division, 545 US 231, 162 L Ed 2d 196, 125 S Ct 2317 (The United States Supreme Court June 13, 2005).
Olmstead v. United States, 72 LED 944, 277 U.S. 438 (The Supreme Court 1928). (1961). Justice 89.
Ruffin v. Commonwealth, 62 Va 790, 796 (Supreme Court of Virginia 1871).
South Carolina v. Katzenbach, 383 U.S. 301, at 311–312, 86 S.Ct. 803 15 L.Ed. 2d 769 (The Supreme Court March 7, 1966).
Stone v. Powell, 49 L.Ed 2d 1067, 428 U.S. 465 (The Supreme Court 1976).
Wolffv. Mcdonnell, 418 US 539, 41 L.Ed 2d 935, 94 S.Ct 2963 (U.S. Supreme Court June 26, 1974).

9. *On Crime and Deviance*

SEAN SWAIN

In my own experience, it is often incredibly difficult to have a productive dialogue on the topics of crime, justice, and punishment, because the ideas swirling around these words are so loaded. The word "crime" conjures to mind bewildering and savage images of murder and rape; the word "justice" invokes a courtroom with a judge in robes, pounding a gavel; and the word "punishment" equates with dark, dreary cell blocks where an arm dangles listlessly from between the bars as a uniformed guard with a baton menacingly patrols the cat-walk. We so thoroughly identify with these representations and the preconceived ideas that accompany the words crime, justice, and punishment that it becomes almost impossible to imagine alternatives outside this socially constructed reality.

Before we can discuss alternatives to our current reality or leap to contemplating some future, crimeless utopia where the carceral state has been dismantled and replaced by free human beings working collectively to solve social problems, we first need to begin by talking about "crime." And before we can really talk about "crime" in an analytical way, we need to define it.

For our purposes here, all visions of murder and mayhem notwithstanding, I would suggest to you that "crime" as a general category of human behavior has two elements. If you lack these elements, you do not have "crime." The first element is "deviant conduct." What I mean by deviant conduct is that for any behavior to be criminal, it has to be perceived as a kind of departure or divergence from what is accepted as the norm. That is to say, we criminalize the deviation, not the norm. We do not criminalize, for instance, helping a little old lady across the street. The reason is, we like to think that assisting the elderly is a norm, a behavior we seek to encourage, not discourage. Rather, we criminalize smacking a little old lady in the head with a two-by-four and stealing her purse. We live in a world where we would like to think that assaulting and robbing the elderly is a deviation from the norm, and so we criminalize such behavior. Consequently, as a first element, "crime" is deviance, deviation—the commission of an act that violates a perceived social norm.

But, not all deviance is criminal. Sticking your tongue out at a sibling in the backseat of the car is deviant. We know it violates a perceived social norm, which is why we never do it when mom is looking in the rearview mirror, for fear of getting caught. We know we are not supposed to do it. But, the deviance of sticking out our tongues at our siblings is not criminal; police never hauled us away and imprisoned us for doing it.

One of the most well-known sets of social norms is the Ten Commandments. Many people ascribe to the Ten Commandments as a model for living. Currently, few of the prohibitions contained in the Ten Commandments are criminalized. Murder, for example, is considered a crime. But lying—bearing false witness—is perfectly legal. So is adultery or worshiping multiple gods or coveting a neighbor's significant other.

It can be argued that lying and committing adultery and coveting a neighbor's house is deviant conduct and that these behaviors are incredibly disruptive to the social order. One could argue that lying, adultery, and coveting, which are not criminal, are more disruptive than criminalized behaviors like jay-walking or spitting on the sidewalk. Yet lying, adultery, and coveting are not criminal because they lack the necessary second element. In order for perceived deviance to be a crime, it must be designated as "punishable" by those who assume the "right to rule."

To be clear, it is not good enough that you or I draw up a laundry list of "annoying things that people do," and that we suggest what we think ought to be done to the people who do those things. That will not make the behaviors "crime." Those behaviors only become "crime" if those who assume the "right to rule" engage their official powers in order to declare that those deviant behaviors are punishable. Only when those who assume the "right to rule" declare that a certain deviant behavior is punishable does "deviance" become "crime."

This gives us a decent, working definition of "crime," and it also gives us a kind of analytical framework in which to think about "crime" and all of the associated topics that come along with it. "Crime," by what we already discussed, is conduct perceived to be deviant that has been designated as punishable by those who assume the "right to rule."

Having established this working definition, there are now a number of implications with respect to this definition that we need to briefly consider. First, when talking about "crime," we are not talking about all deviance. As already discussed, lying, adultery, coveting, and sticking out your tongue at a sibling are all arguably deviant but are still not included in the category of "crime." So, "crime" is a relatively small fraction of the larger category of human behavior perceived to be deviant. Second, not all crime is disruptive and not all disruptive behavior is crime. In some jurisdictions, sodomy—even among married, consenting adults in the privacy of their own bedroom—is outlawed. Reasonably, there is no conceivable argument to support the regulation of sexual conduct between two married, consenting adults in the privacy of their own bedroom on the basis of social disruption. Sometimes, conduct that is objectively accepted as non-disruptive is criminalized.

Simultaneously, the opposite is also true. Consider, on more than one occasion, predatory banking practices have utterly destroyed the global economy, and yet predatory banking practices have never been criminalized. Given the devastation caused by bankers, a valid and reasonable argument can be made that it should be illegal to run a bank rather than rob one. Yet, bank robbers remain locked up while bank managers do not. Go figure.

The point is, some behavior that is not disruptive, in any way, is criminalized, while other behavior that is obviously and undeniably disruptive is not criminalized. Further, consider also that in one day in the nineteenth century in the American South, it was a crime in the early part of the day to assist a slave master's "property" to escape, while, later in that same day, it became a crime for those same slaves to be considered slaves. Escape from slavery was a crime at the start of the day and slavery itself was a crime at the end of the day. So, contrary to the false belief that what gets defined as crime somehow corresponds to some fixed set of lofty moral principles, just the opposite is true. What is included or excluded from the category of behavior we call crime is determined by the sensibilities and whims of those who assume the "right to rule," and those sensibilities and whims can change from year to year, week to week, or even hour to hour.

As a practical matter, we know well why it is that those assuming the "right to rule" have ever-changing sensibilities: those who assume the "right to rule" invariably serve the interests of the privileged elite. Those who assume the "right to rule" get elected or appointed, and they end up taking their marching orders not from voting majorities but from the privileged few who possess political clout and massive wealth.

We know that those with social influence and with large bank accounts seek to keep their influence and money. The easiest way for the influential and wealthy to ensure the continuation of influence and wealth is to make sure that those who assume the "right to rule"—the legislators, judicial officials, and heads of state—write and pass and interpret laws in ways most favorable to the influential and wealthy. The wealthy and powerful influence those who assume the "right to rule," leaving the invisible and impoverished to fend for themselves. As a consequence, bank robbers go to jail while bank managers do not. The slave-owning aristocracy had their interests served right up until northern industrialists with more wealth and influence persuaded those who assumed the "right to rule" to change the laws. And even today, the consideration of which deviant behaviors are most disruptive to society are not as important to those who assume the "right to rule" as placating the desires and needs of the wealthy elite. The recent federal appointments to key regulatory and justice department agencies demonstrates the claim that law is made for the elite by the influence of the elite.

Given these facts, I think we can begin to ponder some interesting observations. The reality that confronts us related to the determination of what constitutes "crime" and what does not is that those who assume the "right to rule" fashion the criminal codes not in order to serve the safety and security concerns of society or to serve the interests of the general welfare, but to preserve the interests of the privileged elite. In light of this, the laws that regulate our behavior are really demands issued on behalf of the privileged elite made into legal statues by those who assume the "right to rule." Likewise, the punishments prescribed for our refusal to meet those demands are really "threats" issued by those who assume the "right to rule," threats issued on behalf of the perceived interests of the privileged elite. The demands and threats that comprise the criminal codes are designed to maintain the status quo, to preserve the influence of wealth and power for those making the demands and threats. Furthermore, the legal system assures that those who do not have influence and wealth are subjected to the demands and threats made by those who have influence and wealth by using the state's monopoly on violence to enforce the will of the powerful.

In short, those who have a monopoly on influence, wealth and power use the criminal codes as a tool to keep the rest of us in our places, to maintain our obedience to their system, to compel our conformity to a set of behaviors that has, for thousands of years, perpetuated wealth for the wealthy and power for the powerful. Somehow, the great majority of us have been persuaded to identify with the continuation of this larger program even though, by any reasonable analysis, the larger program is a vast and monumental swindle, with the great majority of us being the swindled.

It is in this context of these undeniable facts that I propose that there is only one way to completely eliminate "crime." I would further suggest that not only is there only one method for completely eliminating "crime," but that, additionally, if we are serious and sincere in our commitment to eradicating "crime," we could collectively accomplish that goal in less than fifteen minutes. To abolish "crime"—that is, perceived deviance designated as punishable by those who assume the "right to rule"—we need only eliminate the special category of the privileged elite and the special category of those who assume the "right to rule." If we eliminate both of these categories—those who assume the right to rule and privileged elite—there would be no one empowered to distinguish deviance that is not punishable from deviance that is. If there is no one to declare which instances of deviance is punishable, the category of behavior we now know as "crime" ceases to exist.

"Crime"—deviance designated by those who assume the "right to rule" as punishable—vanishes as soon as there no longer exists anyone with the imagined "right to rule" to designate what is punishable. Admittedly, the existence of deviance may well continue, but the elimination of deviance is a separate question from the question of eliminating "crime." We have not yet discussed the elimination of deviance, and thus far have focused exclusively on the elimination of "crime," which, as I described, can be accomplished in less than fifteen minutes. The elimination of "crime" by eradicating influence, wealth, and power would also likely decrease the instance of social deviance, as the elimination of wealth and power monopolies would likely eliminate those social and political forces that drive many people to deviant behavior in the first place. More on the elimination of deviance in a moment, once we dispose entirely of the legal concept of crime.

From a purely anarchist—and, I believe, rational—perspective, the only way to eliminate "crime" is to eradicate influence, wealth, and the imagined "right to rule." To address the problem in any other way is disingenuous. To address the problem in any other way is to suggest that we can develop a method for assessing deviant behavior that defends influence, wealth, and power, which, in turn, presupposes that we ought to develop a method for assessing deviant behavior that defends influence, wealth, and power and that we have some interest in doing so. I reject that presupposition. I would suggest that we should dedicate none of our mental or imaginative resources to address the problems of this larger program, this vast and monumental swindle where demands and threats keep the great majority of us dragging stones up the side of some greed baron's pyramid. I have absolutely no interest in solving problems that contribute to the preservation of a system where those who possess influence, wealth, and power can pass those advantages down to their children and their children's children at the expense of our children, and our children's children.

Knowing that those with influence, wealth, and power and those with an imagined "right to rule" will never willingly relinquish those benefits without a fight, the implication of such an approach is that transformation of this social disorder invariably requires recourse to direct political action. I am not advocating violence, but merely making a practical observation that those with influence, wealth, and the imagined "right to rule" never cede such privilege without bloodshed. That is, after all, the reason why the state has Apache attack helicopters.

Apologists for the existing system and program, the vast and monumental swindle forcing the great majority of us to serve the interests of the privileged few, will object to what I propose. They will assert that we need those exercising the "right to rule" and their laws to protect us from "crime." They will argue that elimination of the state and its protection of wealth and power will result in the sky falling, in the world ending. They will scream that we will have mayhem, havoc, chaos and madness, ignoring the fact that the state's hierarchal program has brought us all of that and worse.

Despite the apologists' hysterical protestations, the fact of the matter is that no law has ever protected anyone from anything. We have criminalized murder for millennia and yet, daily, for thousands of years, humans have killed one another wantonly. We have long outlawed theft but still live in a world where everyone has locks on their doors, often more than one and for good reason. The United States specifically has waged a concerted "war" on drugs for decades and yet the evening news consistently reports that heroin overdoses around the country have become an epidemic, setting records from previous years for overdose deaths.

It would appear from thousands of years of abysmal failure in regulating human behavior that the passage of laws in no way prohibits humans from committing the acts that have been outlawed. In fact, the situation is quite the opposite. It seems the more we promulgate laws and statutes and the more we punish deviance, the more that deviance seems to multiply. There are certainly plenty of laws in the US and the U.S. incarcerates more people per capita than any other country in the world. It would seem more laws and more punishment increase the occurrence of deviance rather than decrease it. Prohibition in the U.S. did not stop people from drinking and the criminalization of narcotics has not stopped people from using drugs. It is a well understood fact that alcohol and drug prohibition are largely responsible for the rise of organized crime in the U.S.

Despite the fact that more law leads to more crime, apologists for the state vehemently object to the abolition of government and of the laws that defend the status quo in spite of the evidence that law has never eliminated crime. Attempting to persuade us that the solution to the problem is more of the same is logically flawed. More laws lead to more crime, so the creation of more laws leads to more crime. Somehow the solution to the problem is more of the problem. Apologists for the state will assert that the abolition of privilege, power, and the carceral state will never work. It should be pointed out that the majority of human history has existed without states. Humans have lived for the vast majority of human existence in small, localized communities that operated mostly by consensus and in the absence of institutionalized hierarchical structures and did so sustainably and successfully (Wells, 2010; Zerzan, 1994). This is more than we can say about our current system. For tens of thousands of years, humans in semi-nomadic hunter-gathering communities never built prisons nor had locks on their doors, and experienced far less social disruption as a consequence of deviance. Being just a few thousand years old, the hierarchical state constitutes far less than one percent of human existence and is seemingly unraveling under the pressures created by overwhelming amounts of social disorder and deviance.

I am not suggesting that we should all run off into the woods to reconnect with our "inner savage," whatever that means, but simply to point out that generally non-hierarchical social structures have always produced fewer instances of deviance than hierarchical systems. In hierarchical systems, the privileged few invariably exploit the many as is demonstrated by the social, political, and economic disparity that exists between the privileged few and the exploited many. In communities where everyone is offered a viable sense of meaning, purpose and connection, rather than compulsion, drudgery and alienation, people behave as if they are more invested in their community's well-being and their rates of deviance greatly diminish. If we hasten the collapse of the current system, which is reasonably in our own best interests, what would a world without privilege and power look like? How would we address disruptive deviance without recourse to criminal codes, courts and prisons?

It is impossible to predict how all seven and one-half billion humans currently inhabiting the earth would exercise the fullness of freedom. I can no more predict how you or anyone else will respond to a world where you are fully responsible for yourself than I can predict what you will do tomorrow when you wake up to confront a world where you are under the regulation and surveillance of strangers who demand your obedience to their inimical program. We can only know that if the current system collapses, in the absence of top-down authority and centralized systems of control, we would have a situation where, as the Zapatista slogan has described it, "many worlds are possible."

I can describe for you under optimum conditions with like-minded people how I would respond to disruptive social deviance. In the absence of a state power, no one can predict the multiple and imaginative ways in which people could organize in small, localized communities, and how they would independently balance their own priorities and act out their collective lives, including speculating on all the possible ways in which they may choose to respond to disruptive deviance.

The genus Homo has been around for roughly 2.3 million years or so, most of that time without living in hierarchal states (Wells, 2010). If we were to collectively return to life with the absence of states, then we would have to confront the question of how to address deviance. I am sure through trial and error, over a long period of time, we will figure it out. And if we prove totally incapable—all seven and one-half billion of us—of solving that dilemma, then perhaps our resultant extinction will be well-earned.

References

Wells, S. (2010). *Pandora's seed: the unforeseen cost of civilization.* New York, NY: Random House.

Zerzan, J. (1994). *Future primitive and other essays.* Columbia, MO: C.A.L. Press.

Contributors

Luis A. Fernandez, Ph.D., is a professor in the Department of Criminology and Criminal Justice at Northern Arizona University. He is the author and editor of several books, *including Policing Dissent, Contemporary Anarchist Studies,* and *Shutting Down the Streets.* His work also appears in various book chapters and journals, including *Social Justice, Contemporary Political Theory, Critical Criminology, and Qualitative Sociology.* His most recent research focuses on the alt-right and the emergence of neo-fascism. Fernandez is currently serving as the President of the Society for the Study of Social Problems.

Jeff Ferrell is currently Professor of Sociology at Texas Christian University, USA, and Visiting Professor of Criminology at the University of Kent, UK. He is the author of the books *Crimes of Style, Tearing Down the Streets, Empire of Scrounge*, and, with Keith Hayward and Jock Young, *Cultural Criminology: An Invitation,* winner of the 2009 Distinguished Book Award from the American Society of Criminology's Division of International Criminology. He is also the co-editor of the books *Cultural Criminology, Ethnography at the Edge, Making Trouble, Cultural Criminology Unleashed,* and *Cultural Criminology: Theories of Crime.* Jeff Ferrell is the founding and current editor of the New York University Press book series Alternative Criminology, and one of the founding editors of the *journal Crime, Media, Culture: An International Journal,* winner of the Association of Learned and Professional Society Publishers' 2006 Charlesworth Award for Best New Journal. In 1998 he received the Critical Criminologist of the Year Award from the Division of Critical Criminology of the American Society of Criminology.

Maurice L. Graham is a coordinator with Save the Kids, writer with Wisdom Behind the Walls, and is currently a prisoner in Minnesota, United States.

Colleen Hackett is Assistant Professor of Sociology at Colorado State University Pueblo. She writes about and organizes against the carceral state and gendered violence. She facilitates a prisoner-led group for prisoners with histories of intimate partner violence at a women's prison and co-edits an anti-authoritarian prisoner publication by and for prisoners identifying as women, trans, and/or gender-nonconforming entitled Unstoppable! publication.

Laura Magnani is Interim Regional Director for the American Friends Service Committee, Pacific Mountain Region. Most of her work, going back to the 1970s, has been in the area of criminal justice. She is author of *America's First Penitentiary: A Two Hundred Year Old Failure* (2000), and *Beyond Prisons: A New Interfaith Paradigm for Our Failed Prison System* (2006, Augsburg/Fortress Press), that analyzes the racial, social and economic underpinnings of the criminal justice system and explores new models of justice. She is also adjunct faculty at Starr King School for the Ministry, a part of the Graduate Theological Union in Berkeley, teaching classes in prisons and restorative justice.

Anthony J. Nocella II, Ph.D., is Assistant Professor of Criminal Justice and Criminology in the Institute for Public Safety at Salt Lake Community College. He is the editor of the *Peace Studies Journal, Poetry Behind the Walls, and Transformative Justice Journal*, along with being a co-editor of five book series including Critical Animal Studies and Theory with Lexington Books and Hip Hop Studies and Activism with Peter Lang Publishing. He is the National Coordinator of Save the Kids, Executive Director of the Institute for Critical Animal Studies, and Director of Academy for Peace Education. He has published over fifty peer-reviewed book chapters or articles and over forty books. He has been interviewed by *Houston Chronicle, Durango Herald, Fresno Bee, Los Angeles Times, Washington Post*, CNN, CBS, Fox, and *New York Times.*

Harold E. Pepinsky is professor emeritus of criminal justice at Indiana University, Bloomington, moving from Worthington, Ohio, to Durango, Colorado, the fall of 2018. His specialty is peacemaking—how to build security and safety in our relations in the face of violence and conflict, instead of punishing offenders. Many of his publications are to be found for download at www.researchgate.org, and www.academia.edu, including *Peacemaking: Reflections of a Radical Criminology* (U. of Ottawa Press, 2006), and with Paul Jesilow, *Myths that Cause Crime* (Seven Locks Press, 3rd edn., 1992; winner of the Academy of Criminal Justice Sciences Outstanding Book Award, 1986).

Reverend David "Wolf Eyes" Rose, Sr. is a coordinator with Save the Kids, writer with Wisdom Behind the Walls, and is currently a prisoner in the United States.

Mark Seis is Associate Professor of Sociology at Fort Lewis College in Durango, Colorado. He has published on a variety of topics ranging from the juvenile death penalty, to environmental topics including the Clean Air Act, global warming, ozone depletion, and acid rain, to various types of environmental crime, to globalization and the environment, to issues concerning radical environmentalism. His primary research interests include sustainable communities, all things environment, anarchist studies, and radical pedagogy.

Jeff Shantz is an engaged activist scholar who has taught anarchist theories and practices in a variety of university classes and community-based courses, and who has decades of community organizing experience within social movements. He currently teaches critical theory, elite deviance, community and human rights in the Department of Criminology at Kwantlen Polytechnic University in Metro Vancouver, Canada. Shantz is the author of numerous books, including *Commonist Tendencies: Mutual Aid Beyond Communism* (Punctum, 2013), *Green Syndicalism: An Alternative Red/Green Vision* (Syracuse University Press, 2012), and *Constructive Anarchy* (Ashgate, 2010). Shantz is the co-founder of the Critical Criminology Working Group (http://www.radicalcriminology.org/) and the founding editor of the journal Radical Criminology (http://journal.radicalcriminology.org/index.php/rc). Scholarly interests include critical theories, migration, critical surveillance studies, corporate crime, transnational crime, and social movements. Samples of his writing may be found at jeffshantz.ca.

Sean Swain, an anarchist prisoner, has been held hostage by an illegitimate rogue state calling itself "Ohio" since 1991 for a provable non-crime and without a legal conviction or sentence. In 2012, at the direction of the Federal Bureau of Investigation, Sean was ideologically targeted and subjected to a year-long regimen of domestic torture at Mansfield Correctional before being transferred to the super-maximum security facility in Youngstown. Sean contributes a weekly segment on the Final Straw radio show which is now accessible online on the Channel Zero Network. His writings are featured at seanswain.org. In 2017, Sean undertook a 50-day hunger-strike in order to get communications mediums restored that prison officials illegally suspended for more than a year. *Last Act of the Circus Animals*, which he co-wrote with Travis Washington, is now published by Little Black Cart and available wherever good books are stolen.

Ben Turk has been working with prison rebels in Ohio for the last five years, but also touring the country extensively with Insurgent Theatre, an anarchist theatre troupe. He has also been on the organizing committee of the North American ABC Conference for the last three years. Please visit LucasvilleAmnesty.org, SupportPrisonerResistance.net and InsurgentTheatre.org for more information.

Index

J

K

M

O

P

Q

R

S

T

Y

Z

RADICAL ANIMAL STUDIES
AND TOTAL LIBERATION

Anthony J. Nocella II, SERIES EDITOR

The **Radical Animal Studies and Total Liberation** book series branches out of Critical Animal Studies (a field co-founded by Anthony J. Nocella II) with the argument that criticism is not enough. Action must follow theory. This series demands that scholars are engaged with their subjects both theoretically and actively via radical, revolutionary, intersectional action for total liberation. Founded in anarchism, the series provides space for scholar-activists who challenge authoritarianism and oppression in their many daily forms. **Radical Animal Studies and Total Liberation** promotes accessible and inclusive scholarship that is based on personal narrative as well as traditional research, and is especially interested in the advancement of interwoven voices and perspectives from multiple radical, revolutionary social justice groups and movements such as Black Lives Matter, Idle No More, Earth First!, the Zapatistas, ADAPT, prison abolition, LGBTTQQIA rights, disability liberation, Earth Liberation Front, Animal Liberation Front, political prisoners, radical transnational feminism, environmental justice, food justice, youth justice, and Hip Hop activism.

To order other books in this series please contact our Customer Service Department:

(800) 770-LANG (within the US)
(212) 647-7706 (outside the US)
(212) 647-7707 FAX

To find out more about the series or browse a full list of titles, please visit our website:

WWW.PETERLANG.COM

www.ingramcontent.com/pod-product-compliance
Ingram Content Group UK Ltd.
Pitfield, Milton Keynes, MK11 3LW, UK
UKHW020842290926
15470UKWH00004B/1497

9 781433 158001